P9-AQZ-273

HUMAN FACTORS OF THE USER-SYSTEM INTERFACE

A Report on an ESPRIT Preparatory Study

HUMAN FACTORS OF THE USER-SYSTEM INTERFACE

A Report on an ESPRIT Preparatory Study

Edited by

Bruce CHRISTIE
ITT Europe Human Factors Technology Centre
Harlow, Essex, United Kingdom

1985

NORTH-HOLLAND
AMSTERDAM • NEW YORK • OXFORD

ISBN: 0 444 87832 7

Published by:

ELSEVIER SCIENCE PUBLISHERS B.V.
P.O. Box 1991
1000 BZ Amsterdam
The Netherlands

for:

THE COMMISSION OF THE EUROPEAN COMMUNITIES
Directorate-General Information Market and Innovation
Boîte Postale 1907
Luxembourg

Sole distributors for the U.S.A. and Canada:

ELSEVIER SCIENCE PUBLISHING COMPANY, INC.
52 Vanderbilt Avenue
New York, N.Y. 10017
U.S.A.

Library of Congress Cataloging-in-Publication Data

Main entry under title:

Human factors of the user-system interface.

Published for the Commission of the European Communities, Directorate-General Information Market and Innovation.
Bibliography: p.
Includes index.
1. Electronic data processing--Research--European Economic Community countries. 2. Human engineering. 3. Man-machine systems. 4. European Strategic Programme of Research and Development in Information Technology. I. Christie, Bruce. II. European Strategic Programme of Research and Development in Information Technology.
QA76.27.H85 1985 004'.01'9 85-20707
ISBN 0-444-87832-7 (U.S.)

PRINTED IN THE NETHERLANDS

PREFACE

This book does not attempt to be a comprehensive account of Human Factors in Information Technology, nor an in-depth textbook. What it does do is provide a distillation of the views of two industry-based groups with a practical interest in seeing appropriate human factors research done to the benefit of the Information Technology Industry in Europe. It should be of interest to anyone interested in ESPRIT, in Human Factors under ESPRIT, in the application of Human Factors or in Information Technology from the user's point of view.

The book is an edited version of an ESPRIT Preparatory Study entitled "Human Factors of the User-System Interface". ESPRIT is the European Strategic Programme of Research and development in Information Technology, a ten-year transnational programme funded jointly by European Industry and the Commission of the European Communities, the first main studies of which were launched in 1984. The Preparatory Studies helped in the development of the framework for the Programme.

ESPRIT is aimed at encouraging pre-competitive research in Information Technology, bringing together industrial and academic researchers in different Member States to focus on research and development that will contribute significantly to the growth of the Information Technology Industry in Europe. Human Factors is recognised as having an important part to play in this.

The Preparatory Study on "Human Factors of the User-System Interface" was a joint project by the Human Factors Technology Centre (now part of ITT Europe's ESC Research Centre in Harlow, U.K., but under the aegis of Standard Telecommunication Laboratories at the time of the study) and Softlab in Munich, F.R. Germany. The work was done during the period January through April 1983.

The original authors of the study (in alphabetical order) were:

Human Factors Technology Centre:

- Alberdi, Marco de
- Christie, Bruce
- Harvey, James
- Kaiser, Polly M.
- Lansdale, Mark
- McEwan, John
- Ottley, Sue

Softlab:

- Franck, Reinhold
- Schroeder, Klaus
- Schubert, Axel
- Stephan, Bernd

The authors benefitted from discussions with a number of other people, including the following (in alphabetical order):

Dr Jack Field
Survey Research Unit
The Open University

Professor Anthony Gale
Department of Psychology
Southampton University

Mr Kofer
Siemens Research Centre
Munich

Professor K.P. Lohr
Bremen University

Mr Mangold and Mr Schurmann
AEG-Telefunken Research Centre
Ulm

The original authors are grateful to these people for their various contributions to the team's thinking and accept responsibility for any misinterpretations of the inputs provided.

Background discussions with a number of other people were also helpful, including:

Dr Stuart Card
Xerox Palo Alto Research Center

Professor Alphonse Chapanis
Communications Research Laboratory
The Johns Hopkins University

Dr Koichi Furukawa
Institute for New Generation Computer Technology
Tokyo

Jeffrey Galvin
Apple Computers
California

Professor Donald Michie
Department of Machine Intelligence
University of Edinburgh

Peter Morse
Apple Computers (U.K.)

Professor Nicholas Negroponte and
Dr Richard Bolt
Massachussetts Institute of Technology

Dr Cynthia Solomon
Atari, Inc.
Cambridge, Massachussetts

Dr Robert Spence
Department of Electrical Engineering
Imperial College of Science and Technology

Dr Bonnie Lynn Webber
Department of Computer and Information Sciences
University of Pennsylvania

In addition to the background discussions, the authors were fortunate in being able to see a variety of products, including the following.

CAMIC/S was presented by colleagues at SOFTLAB GMBH.

BITSY OF TRIUMPH-ADLER AG was presented by DR. RICHTMANN+EDER.

The system IBM 5520 was presented by IBM DEUTSCHLAND GMBH.

The accounting package FIBU was presented by THOMAS KOCH - COMPUTER VERTRIEBS GMBH on a COBOS computer of DeTeWe.

LISA was evaluated on the basis of a demonstration given to STL by Apple Computer and Apple Computer (UK) Ltd., a presentation to softlab by APPLE COMPUTER MARKETING GMBH, and a review of the literature.

The translation system LOGOS was presented by LOGOS COMPUTER SYSTEMS DEUTSCHLAND GMBH.

WANG's OIS 145 was presented by WANG DEUTSCHLAND GMBH.

PET/MAESTRO by SOFTLAB.

ICL's PERQ system was presented by QUITE BRICK COMPUTERGESELLSCHAFT.

STAR was evaluated on the basis of a presentation by RANK XEROX GMBH, another presentation by SIEMENS and a review of the literature.

The word processing package WORDSTAR was presented by THOMAS KOCH - COMPUTER VERTRIEBS GMBH on a COBOS computer of DeTeWe.

Product information was provided by:

AEG-TELEFUNKEN (speech and readers)
INTERSTATE ELECTRONICS CORPORATION (speech)
OLIVETTI (ergonomics of the hardware)
TELESENSORY SPEECH SYSTEMS (speech)

A set of lectures about the design of an ergonomic system at the SCHWEIZERISCHE BANKVEREIN provided valuable insights. Results from research commissioned by the Rationalisierungs-Kuratorium der Deutschen Wirtschaft e.V. were kindly made available.

The chapter on "species of interaction" in particular benefitted from attendance at the following conferences:

Office Automation Conference, February 21-23 Philadelphia, USA

Hanover Fair, April 15-20, Hanover Germany

Intergraphics 83, April 11-14, Tokyo, Japan.

The book provides a distillation of the work done by the team. It attempts to keep to the original report as closely as possible, consistent with making stylistic changes and providing some updates where appropriate. The editor accepts responsibility for any misinterpretation or other mistreatment of the original text.

Further information about ESPRIT can be obtained from the Commission of the European Communities Information Technologies and Telecommunications Task Force, provisional address: Rue de la Loi 200, B-1049 Brussels.

CONTENTS

CHAPTER 1:

INTRODUCTION

GENERAL BACKGROUND - THE ESPRIT PROGRAMME

We are living through exciting times, times of change. It has been clear for some time that our society has been moving on from a society in which agriculture predominated, through a society in which the emphasis was on the manufacturing industries, to the dawn of a new society in which the emphasis is shifting very markedly towards the information-intensive sectors, eg. banking, insurance, consultancy services, and other services where the main activity is the handling of information. This is our "information society", a product of our scientific, technical and political history, enabled by the "microchip revolution".

We can expect many changes, affecting all aspects of our everyday lives. The personal computers we can buy in high street shops, the automatic service tills at banks, the teletext and videotex services now available, the word processors that are becoming a feature of many offices, videotaperecorders, "talking cars" - these are just the very earliest signs of the new Information Technology (IT) that will change our lives in the years ahead. Information Technology offers many benefits for business and industry. By providing automatic customer services available from home at the touch of a button twenty-four hours a day, seven days a week, it improves access to consumers. The service engineer who calls to repair a complex piece of industrial equipment can be provided with electronic manuals and "expert systems" that will help to diagnose the problem and provide a step by step guide through the solution. Electronic directories provide more comprehensive, more up to date, and more accessible information about what is on offer and who can supply it. Faster and more reliable checking of credit, invoicing, and electronic funds transfer improve organizational response time to the needs of customers. Faster response and higher quality, more reliable information improve the company's image. Cleaner, quieter, better designed work environments, coupled with more challenging but less stressful work, improve the well-being of staff. These are just some of the benefits to be gained through an intelligent application of the new technology.

The benefits extend beyond business and industry. In the educational sector, the new technology offers more personalized direct tuition. It makes educational possibilities available to more people for a greater part of our lives, by means of personal computers, telecommunications, videodiscs, optical discs, and technology yet to come. It provides an opportunity for more people to have access to very sophisticated machines that can handle relatively routine and well-defined operations, enabling us to concentrate on developing higher-order concepts and problem-solving skills. It impacts our health services in many ways, improving access to people needing care by providing communications into the home for emergency and monitoring purposes, improving the match between services offered and health needs, improving individual treatment for example by providing electronic "expert systems" to support medics and paramedics, and improving the efficiency of health administration. For the person at home, as well as providing shopping, health and educational services into the home, the technology provides a wider range of entertainment possibilities based on satellite and cable communications, personal computers, and other technology, and it aids in the day to day running of the home by providing electronic control of the use of energy and other resources and computer support in the management of finances and other aspects of running a home. These are just some of the benefits on offer to us if we harness the potential of the new technology and use it to our genuine advantage.

Annual world sales of Information Technology (IT) products are forecast to be in the region of 100 000 million ECUs (about £60 000 million). The European market accounts for between 20% and 33% of this, depending on the particular sector (33% of the £17 000 million telecommunications market, 25% of the £35 000 million data processing systems market, and 20% of the £3 000 million integrated circuit market). Simply on this basis one might expect European industry to take between 20% and 33% of the market share. As of January 1983 this had not been the case, however. European industry had in fact taken only about 10% of the market share. It had failed to grasp the opportunity.

This failure can be traced in part to the difficulties of operating across national and cultural boundaries. Yet it is important to do so. Home markets do not offer a sufficient base for the innovation and flexibility that are needed in this industry, where developments occur so rapidly that products often become obsolete almost as soon as they are launched. Large scale investment is needed that often goes beyond the resources of any one nation. And research and development needs to be efficient. Europe cannot afford too much duplication of effort among member countries.

These difficulties have contributed to Europe's overall trade deficit in IT products, and its relatively poor performance in the registering of patents. The result is that Community industry has been losing the race to create a solid IT base, and has had to rely too much on importing foreign products, mainly from the United States and Japan.

The European Commission has been warning of the situation for around ten years and has taken several initiatives to try and redress the imbalance. Euronet-DIANE, INSIS and CADDIA are examples of its successes in developing information exchange systems within the Community, but outside of this area progress has been slow until recently when the launching of the ESPRIT programme marked a potential breakthrough.

ESPRIT is the European Strategic Programme of Research in Information Technology. The guidelines for the programme were adopted by the Council of Ministers in June 1982 who on the 4th of November of that year gave the go-ahead for a series of pilot projects that would start in 1983/4 and pave the way for the main programme starting in 1984/5.

The aim of the ESPRIT programme is to lay the basis for Community industry to be in the forefront of innovation in the 1990s rather than lagging behind. The success of the programme will depend on the degree to which it can foster cooperation between different companies operating in different member states. So far the signs are encouraging. European companies from the member states have seconded around one hundred experts to work with the Commission in helping to launch ESPRIT, and the wider industrial and academic communities have also made positive contributions through working groups, and in other ways.

The strategy of ESPRIT is directed to the future, concentrating on stimulating precompetitive research in five key areas:

- Advanced microelectronics where Very Large Scale Integration (VLSI) technology will make a positive contribution towards improving system performance whilst reducing costs.

- Software Technology where the market for system software is growing at 32% a year and that for applications software at 49% a year.

- Computer Integrated Manufacturing where integrated system architecture, general software development, machine control and development of sensors and microelectronic sub-systems will contribute to the systematic computerization of the manufacturing process.

- Advanced Information Processing including the development of techniques in such areas as signal processing, natural language interfaces, and expert systems.

- Office Systems which is expected to become the largest single market within Information Technology and where the ESPRIT research will focus on the user interface.

The level of effort needed in order to make significant progress in these areas is high. The overall ESPRIT budget (over five years) is approximately £900 million, half of which is to be provided by the Community and half by industry.

Further information about the ESPRIT programme in general is provided by Cadiou (1985) and Carpentier (1985).

As part of the preparation for the ESPRIT programme a set of Preparatory Studies were commissioned covering the key areas. These were done in order to review the state of the art in each of the areas concerned and to define the key issues and areas of research that would need to be addressed under the main programme. This book is one of a series that presents the results of those Preparatory Studies, in this case the one concerned with Human Factors of the User-System Interface.

THE HUMAN FACTORS CRITERION

The Information Technology industry is a dynamic, fast-moving high technology sector. Its rapid and continuing generation of advanced technology products makes it a key factor in promoting economic and social development. The rate of change is so great that around half the products on the market now did not exist even three years ago.

The rate of change shows no signs of slowing down. New technologies are making possible increases in circuit speed and chip densities that will reduce even further the cost of memory devices whilst improving performance and extending the range of capabilities that products can offer.

It is already evident that this trend has been leading to products that are highly competitive in terms of their cost, the capabilities they offer the user (e.g. power typing, filing, communications, and so on), and their physical parameters (e.g. amount of memory).

It is also evident that these products have so far failed to adapt adequately in terms of the user-system interface and the needs of the new types of user. The users of office automation products typically are not computer specialists. The traditional kinds of user-system dialogues used in conventional computer systems can be powerful demotivators in the office environment, causing users to reject new systems. There is an urgent need to develop methods of user-system communication that are better suited to the needs of the new types of user. Any product to make a significant step forward in this regard will inevitably improve its competitive position considerably as long as costs and capabilities also remain competitive.

The human factors of the user-system interface still reflect too much the pre-history of information technology in data processing systems. The new users of information technology - in the office, in the home, and elsewhere - are not computer specialists and do not wish to become so just in order to be able to use the new products. As well as low cost, high capability, reliability, and so on, users are increasingly demanding high quality in the human factors of the user-system interface. It is in this area more than any other that the competition will be waged. No matter what progress Europe may make on other aspects of information technology, it will lose the race unless it takes steps to meet the human factors criterion as well.

A Definition of Human Factors

The term "human factors" in this context refers to all the aspects of using a system that affect what users understand about the system, how they feel about the system, and how they behave in regard to the system (including willingness to use it and their performance when using it). The term is also used to refer to the research and development activities associated with these.

Human Factors has various historical, conceptual and methodological links with a number of other disciplines. One of its roots has been in industrial design; here, the questions addressed by classical ergonomics (e.g. concerning the physical layout of components of a workstation) form a natural extension of mainstream industrial design. Another historical root has been in mainstream cognitive psychology; here, the models of cognitive processing developed by psychologists to explain and predict behaviour generally can make a powerful contribution to the design of the user interface, especially in regard to the "logic" of the design of the operating procedures. Another important link is with artificial intelligence, where attempts to build "intelligence" into the system can make use of the models developed within cognitive psychology, both in order to mimick relevant aspects of human behaviour and in order to achieve a degree of "cognitive compatibility" between the artifically "intelligent" system and the truly intelligent human.

In addition to these links, there are a number of others. Psychophysiology, for example, has made important contributions to our understanding of the physiological and other responses of the individual to the demands made by different working environments. In the case of electronic systems, this has led to the introduction of national and international ergonomic standards and guidelines (e.g. concerning the design of visual display units) which must be met if products are to be acceptable in the countries concerned. A complementary example is social and organizational psychology where a vast body of research is available on the psychology of people in groups as this relates to organizational effectiveness. Here, the implications for the design of electronic systems largely await systematic description.

There are other links as well but these are sufficient to illustrate that human factors is not an island of research and development that is quite separate from other disciplines. On the contrary, it is rich in links with other bodies of knowledge and, whilst a young offspring, can look for important theoretical and methodological support from its parents and siblings.

Approaches to Human Factors

The work done on the Preparatory Study on which this book is based, including a review of the research being done in key centres around the world, highlighted the fact that different approaches to improving the human factors of the user-system interface can be developed and have been adopted by different groups.

The work of any particular group typically combines more than one approach, although in different mixes. Rather than discuss the different groups individually it will be more useful in this brief account to organise the discussion around the key dimensions that seem, admittedly subjectively, to emerge from the variety of work going on.

<u>The concrete versus the abstract</u>. It is perhaps not entirely irrelevant that human thinking at least in some important respects seems to move from the concrete to the more abstract during the course of development. Children seem to move through a stage of thinking in terms of "concrete operations" earlier than they attain "abstract operations". At the level of our species, it seems (from our point of view, at least) that the apes (the purported modern day equivalents of our ancestors) think in more concrete terms than we do.

It may be that adults may sometimes find it easier to absorb new ideas if they are presented initially in concrete rather than abstract terms. Certainly, the notion of providing plenty of "for instances" seems a popular rule of thumb in management consultancy, and the use of metaphor and analogy which is characteristic of some approaches to psychotherapy may serve to facilitate communication by (amongst other things) making it more concrete.

The Xerox Star and its various derivatives (e.g. Apple Lisa and Macintosh) may not represent the <u>best</u> approach to the user-system interface but they have helped to promote the cause of human factors by making abstract notions of "user friendliness", "ease of use", and so on, more concrete. They are concrete examples of what can be done (though not by any means of <u>everything</u> that can be done). They are real products, really on the market. This may in some ways be worth more than many erudite publications in professional journals discussing human factors issues in more abstract ways.

The Star and related products are also concrete in another way. They do not require the user to interact with information in the abstract. They provide the user with concrete images with which to work. This does not necessarily mean that the Star type of approach is the best. The use of concrete images may help the person to whom electronic information systems represent a very new field, but - just as the child moves on from concrete operations to abstract operations as his or her competence develops - so the office worker of tomorrow may well outgrow the use of concrete operations at the user-system interface. The use of such images may well prove too constraining, and just as the child moves beyond the limitations of "concrete operations" so the skilled office worker may want to break free of constraints imposed by too concrete an approach to the electronic environment.

Demonstrations versus tests. The value of demonstrations can be seen in the work of MIT (Massachussetts Institute of Technology) where the Media Room has provided an environment where new approaches to user-system interaction have been developed, simulated and demonstrated. Whilst the particular concepts presented can be criticised in some respects from the perspective provided by recent developments in human factors thinking, the work in the Media Room caught the imagination at the time it was first presented and was part of the stimulus for developments elsewhere. Many of the ideas in the Xerox Star and related products, as well as in work at Queen Mary College London, Imperial College London, and elsewhere can be seen in the earlier work at MIT.

This simulation work is important in helping to get things moving. It is very closely related to the "imagination games" that people play in other areas and that form such an important part of human psychology. It is a type of fantasy that can stimulate the imagination, just as science fiction can. Concepts such as teleportation ("Beam me down, Scotty"), anti-matter, black holes, white holes, hyperspace, hyperdrive, and so on are familiar concepts to many people today - especially younger people (Star Wars, Close Encounters, Space Invaders, etc). They have caught the imagination and become a kind of reality - part of the mythology of the Twentieth Century - so much so that many people would find difficulty in sorting out the list of concepts given above (teleportation, anti-matter, etc.) into those that are "pure science fiction" and those that are "scientific".

Demonstrations are not usually associated with rigorous tests. Their role is generally taken to be to capture the imagination. This is in contrast to the rigorous scientific work of the university or other laboratory. But imagination can only get us so far. We do need to test it against reality. In Freudian terms, there is more to being human than giving constant free reign to one's Id. The Ego has an important role in human psychology in maintaining a degree of reality-orientation.

Pragmatic versus academic. Much of the work on improving the user-system interface has been driven by pragmatic considerations, chiefly getting together a system that actually does work and is sufficiently useable to be saleable. This has forced some consideration of the user, but traditionally at a rather minimal level.

Whilst computer systems were novel this approach was sufficient. Users were effectively presented with a "take it or leave it" option. If they wanted access to computing power they had to accept the mystique (and downright clumsiness) of the interface. Nowadays, this is no longer sufficient. Computers are not so novel, and users are not so accepting.

The users of the late 1980s and beyond will be very demanding in what they expect of the user-system interface. If a manager's young son or daughter can find playing with an inexpensive computer game easy and fun, why should an expensive office system be difficult and aggravating? So there is an increasing pragmatic need to treat the user-system interface more seriously. The human factors of the user-system interface will increasingly provide the competitive edge.

The academic institutions are not driven by short-term pragmatic motives as much, and are a natural environment for developing the science on which developments in this area need to be based. Unfortunately, the academic institutions are only now beginning to wake up to the fact that the Information Technology Age is dawning, and even now they often have difficulty in prioritizing their research to take account of the rapid developments in technology that are taking place in industry. There is much potential value to be gained in encouraging and facilitating the right kinds of links between industry with its pragmatic perspective and the universities and polytechnics with their academic perspective.

Psychological versus physical. The "physical aspects" of the user-system interface are important and are the most visible. Perhaps one reason they are the most obvious or most readily grasped is because they are concrete. It is very important that the user does not get backache from poor workstation design, or headache from VDU flicker or glare, or develop rashes, or feel dehumanised. It is important that the keyboard layout or design of the speech input device, that the type of screen or type of voice synthesiser used, facilitates rather than hinders high productivity.

These things are important, and much research has been done on the physical aspects so that our understanding of these aspects has developed to a stage where it is even possible to set standards with some degree of confidence. It is now in regard to the psychological aspects of the user-system interface that great strides forward remain to be made, and will be made by the close of the 1980s - either by Europe or by the U.S. or Japan.

It is inconceivable to think of a human to whom his or her psychology is not central. A person without a human psyche (mental world, personality, style of being) is a "vegetable" or "animal", and difficult for other humans to relate to or work with effectively. Neither can we work very well (on business matters or office work) with cats and dogs, even though these biological systems are more sophisticated than any robots built so far. "Sophistication" (of biological systems or electronic systems) is not sufficient. We need to develop electronic systems that have the right sort of psychology, that are psychologically compatible with their human users and complement their users in terms of their capabilities.

The competition for developing the best user-system interface will be won or lost in the area of human-machine psychological compatibility.

OBJECTIVES AND STRUCTURE OF THE BOOK

The book is a vehicle for reporting on the ESPRIT Preparatory Study on Human Factors of the User-System Interface. The study was one of a set of preparatory studies established as preliminaries to a range of Pilot Projects and the subsequent Main Programme which started in 1984.

The Preparatory Study on Human Factors of the User-System Interface started in January 1983 and was completed by 6th May 1983. It was a collaborative venture between the Human Factors Technology Centre in the UK (now part of ITT Europe's ESC Research Centre in Harlow, but under the aegis of Standard Telecommunication Laboratories at the time of the study) and Softlab in Munich, F.R. Germany.

The purpose of the study was to review the state of the art in human factors of the user-system interface in a world context and identify the key issues associated with effective and successful interfaces for electronic systems in office environments.

The study was intended to provide a top-level view, to identify key issues, and to assess the state of the art. It was not intended and it was not possible in the time available to compile an in-depth comprehensive account of research in all relevant areas. This would have needed to have been the subject of a larger project. Specific aims of the study were to :

- Define the nature of the problem, relating it to those areas of office activities and functions which electronic systems could address most profitably in the medium term future (see Chapter 2).

- Describe existing types of user-system interfaces in terms of the human factors aspects of input devices and output media (see Chapter 3).

- Consider the role of the user's model of the system and issues raised by this for interface design (see Chapter 4).

- Examine the human factors aspects of how information is presented and requirements for improving the user-system interface in this regard (see Chapter 5).

Additional aims of the study were to :

- Make recommendations in regard to advancing the state of the art in human factors in Europe (see Chapter 6).

- Identify key research centres within Europe and elsewhere (see Appendix II).

The book is organised around these objectives. In addition, Appendix I provides an outline of subsequent Human Factors work initiated under ESPRIT (as of 1984).

Interest to Psychologists, Ergonomists And Other Human Factors Specialists

Psychology is concerned with what people do, think and feel. It recognises that human behaviour is a function both of the person concerned and of the environment. A person who reports the colour of a disk held against a dark background as being 'white' may report it as being 'grey' when it is held against a white background. A person who can behave effectively and bravely in an emergency such as a fire may need help when faced with a spider in the bath. A person who was effective in the office environment of yesterday may or may not adapt well to the electronic office of the future. The person who had to struggle hard to keep up in yesterday's school may show great talent in the computer-oriented world of tomorrow.

Information technology represents the most significant change in the human environment since the industrial revolution. Any psychologist with the slightest concern for "ecological validity" will see the need to take account of the new "electronic environment" in theory development and experimentation. The changes concerned are especially important because they impact directly on that uniquely human quality which is our ability to communicate. This ability more than any other marks us out from the other animals with whom we share this planet. The psychological aspects of electronic systems have implications for psychologists in different specialist fields, including education, clinical settings, and organizations.

Psychologists are already in a position to answer many of the questions relating to the design of user-oriented interfaces on the basis of existing psychological knowledge, and will make further contributions as many new avenues are opened up for further psychological research.

Ergonomists and other human factors specialists who have traditionally focussed on the more physical aspects of the interface between human and machine are also turning their attention to the new kinds of "machines" with which an increasingly large proportion of the working population work.

Human factors specialists of all sorts have a responsibility to ensure that necessary research is done and that the results of research are made known to manufacturers and others concerned with the development and application of new products. It is especially important that national and international standards are based on adequate research. Standards or guidelines based on inadequate empirical research would be likely to prove damaging rather than helpful.

Interest To Manufacturers

The market for information technology is very large, and office systems are the largest part of it. The industry is rapidly growing, and the rate of change is likely to continue to be high for some time. What products are capable of doing is increasing all the time, in technical terms at least.

This is leading increasingly to a situation where different manufacturers are offering products that are highly competitive in terms of their cost, the capabilities they offer (e.g. communications, power typing, filing, and so on), and their physical parameters (e.g. amount of memory). There is every reason to expect that this trend will continue and that the competition will increase.

In order to capitalize on the huge potential of the emerging technologies, and to realize their benefits in practice, it is essential that they are made accessible to the ordinary person who is interested in taking advantage of the benefits but who does not wish to have to undergo special training in order to do so. The kinds of user-system dialogues that were often used in conventional computer systems can work against acceptance of products in the office environment, causing users to reject the new technology. Any product to make a significant step forward in the human-machine compatibility of the dialogues used for communication between electronic office products and their intended users will inevitably improve its competitive position considerably as long as costs and technical capabilities also remain competitive.

Until very recently, the form of user-system interface used in office products still reflected too much the pre-history of information technology in data processing systems. Some new ideas have begun to emerge, but many more are needed. The new users of information technology - in the home and elsewhere, as well as in the office - are becoming increasingly demanding. As well as requiring low cost, high capability, excellent reliability, and so on, they are increasingly also demanding high quality in the design of the user-system interface.

It is in the design of user-oriented interfaces more than in any other area that the competition for the information technology market will be won or lost.

There is a dual aspect to this. As well as opening up new market possibilities, the new products will have secondary impacts on existing markets. Users' expectations will inevitably be raised by seeing what can be achieved with new products. The manager who sees a child playing happily and easily with a relatively inexpensive computer game will be reluctant to accept that an office product meant to support real business has to be difficult to use. The new products will also open up possibilities for new kinds of services which will also have impacts on existing products. Just as the use of carbon paper has declined since the advent of the convenience photocopier, so electronic copying and distribution of "papers" can be expected to impact the role of the convenience photocopier. Just as the use of telegrams has declined since the voice telephone has become widespread, so the new kinds of products to emerge under the banner of information technology can be expected to stimulate demand for new kinds of services that will impact existing communications systems. These are just examples from a whole range of impacts that can reasonably be expected to become apparent over the coming years.

COMPLEMENTARY BOOKS

There are a number of complementary books which the interested reader may wish to consult, and more are appearing almost weekly. References are given later at appropriate points in the text, but the following are good examples.

Card, S.K., Moran, T.P., & Newell, A. (1983)
The psychology of human-computer interaction. London/New Jersey: Lawrence Erlbaum Associates. The scope of the book is narrower than the title might suggest, concentrating on perceptual-motor and cognitive aspects (especially in regard to text editing) but it is a useful book and provides some interesting insights into some of the research that has been going on at Xerox Palo Alto Research Center.

Christie, B. (1985) (ed.)
Human factors of information technology in the office. Chichester: John Wiley and Sons. Produced by ITT's Human Factors Technology Centre, this book provides an industrial

perspective on the psychology of electronic office systems. The book is divided into four main parts, concerned with: a psychological and historical introductory overview of the office; a review of product trends, focussing on a discussion of the psychology of electronic meeting systems, information systems, and decision systems; a discussion of product usability - how to assess it, and guidelines for achieving it; and a discussion of the factors involved in introducing electronic office systems into an organisation.

Cohen, B.G.F. (1984) (ed.)
Human aspects in office automation. Amsterdam: Elsevier Science Publishers. Five areas are covered: office environmental health issues; work organisational factors; ergonomic aspects of the workplace; physiological and psychological effects of office work; and strategies for alleviating worksite stress.

Doswell, A. (1983)
Office automation. Chichester/New York: John Wiley & Sons. Part of the Wiley Series in Information Processing, this provides a broad overview of the office automation field, covering human factors and other aspects, organised into five main sections: 'concepts', 'office systems', 'applications', and 'implications'.

Feigenbaum, E.A. & McCorduck, P. (1983)
The fifth generation: artificial intelligence and Japan's computer challenge to the world. London/California: Addison-Welsely. This is a very readable book giving an overview of what the Japanese Fifth Generation Computer initiative is about. It contains some useful appendices giving information on key research centres, operational expert systems, and related information.

Jarrett, D. (1982)
The electronic office: a management guide to the office of the future. Aldershot: Gower Publishing Company Ltd. This provides a readable overview of electronic office systems.

Monk, A. (1984)
Fundamentals of human-computer interaction. London: Academic Press. The book is based on a course run for the computer industry by the University of York, aimed primarily at systems designers, programmers and engineers concerned with designing systems for use by humans.

Otway, H.J. & Peltu, M. (1983) (eds.)
New office technology: human and organizational aspects. London: Frances Pinter, for the Commission of the European Communities. This is a publication from the INSIS Programme of the Commission of the European Communities. It provides a useful collection of papers discussing the human and organisational aspects of introducing new office technology into an organisation.

Roukens, J. & Renuart, J.F. (1985)
ESPRIT '84: status report of ongoing work. Amsterdam: North-Holland for the Commission of the European Communities. This book presents a status report on collaborative work done by more than 150 research groups involving European industry and academia, between September 1983 and September 1984, to launch the ESPRIT programme. It covers all aspects of ESPRIT, not just those related to Human Factors.

Sime, M.E. & Coombs, M.J. (1983)
Designing for human-computer communication. London/New York: Academic Press. This is a useful book of readings by key researchers from the U.S., Canada, Sweden, Scotland, and - mostly - England. The book is organised into two main parts,

dealing with 'the user interface' (issues such as natural language, 'user growth', database query) and 'the task interface' (medical consultation, air traffic control, and other application areas).

CHAPTER 2:

DEFINITION OF THE PROBLEM

INTRODUCTION

Information technology promises to provide benefits in the office area, better solutions to the needs that individuals and organisations have in regard to information processing and communication in the office context. This chapter presents a view of what the needs are that office systems must address in order to be successful. It considers these needs in relation to:

- models of user-system interaction
- the psychophysiological context
- the organisational context
- functional analysis and definition of new services
- evaluation of systems.

MODELS OF USER-SYSTEM INTERACTION

This section does not present a model, because no adequate model exists. It is concerned with explaining the need to develop such a model, or set of models, and with indicating the kinds of thing that such a set of models should encompass.

Appropriate models of user-system interaction need to be developed in order that those concerned with research and development can be sure they are talking the same language - that when one person uses the term "goal" it means the same as when another does, and that it relates to other concepts (e.g. "objective") in the same way. Given the ambiguities of everyday parlance, reliance on common-sense definitions of key concepts can only lead to confusion, misunderstandings, and logical inconsistencies.

Models are also needed in order to be able to test ideas systematically and efficiently, so that maximum useful new knowledge is gained for minimum research effort. This is less likely to be achieved if research is guided by intuition and ill-defined "approaches" rather than clearly defined models.

Levels of Modelling

Models can describe user-system interaction at different levels. In terms of Human Factors, the main levels are:

- the physical ergonomic
- the cognitive psychological
- the situational psychological

The physical ergonomic level. This level is arguably the most researched in regard to Information Technology. Well-defined guidelines and standards now exist that provide the product designer with guidance on the physical characteristics of common input devices (especially the design of keyboards), output devices (especially visual displays), and the physical configuration of workstations. Much of the knowledge in this area has been made readily available in such publications as the manual by Cakir *et al*. (1980), Grandjean and Vigliani (1982), and others.

The focus of interest has been largely on issues such as low-level productivity measures (e.g. speed and accuracy of typing), operator satisfaction in terms of expressed preferences, and physiological aspects (the main concerns here being to avoid eye strain, back-ache, damage to the wrists or fingers, and other potential areas of discomfort or injury). F.R. Germany has been among the leaders in terms of developing standards. The trades unions in various countries have actively promoted the adoption of such standards and guidelines, largely under the general umbrella of health and safety considerations, and in general manufacturers have been concerned that their products should comply with standards and guidelines in this area.

<u>The cognitive psychological</u>. Possibly the best-known example of directly relevant modelling at this level is the work by Card, Moran and Newell (1983), based at Xerox Parc. They propose a cognitive model of user-system interaction (the GOMS model) that incorporates four main concepts:

- a set of Goals, which define the state of affairs to be achieved - they are organised hierarchically

- a set of Operators, which are elementary acts which are necessary in order to create a change in the user's mental state and/or the task/system environment - they can be perceptual, motor or cognitive in nature

- a set of Methods for achieving the goals - these are conditional sequences of goals and operators that the user has already learned, not plans that are formulated at the time of executing the task

- and a set of Selection rules for choosing among competing methods - these are of the form, "if such-and-such is true in the current task situation, then use method M".

The GOMS model is a generic model which can be used to generate more specific models at different levels of analysis. Card *et al*. report on how the GOMS model has been applied with some success both to text-editing and other well-structured tasks, and to a semi-creative task (computer-aided circuit design), to predict performance (especially times taken).

The Card *et al*. work, although possibly the best known, is not the only work going on in this area. Two further examples of particular note are:

- the work by Green (at the MRC Applied Psychology Unit in Cambridge, U.K.) and Payne (at the MRC/ESRC Applied Psychology Unit in Sheffield, U.K.) on TAG theory (e.g. Payne, 1984)

- the work on goal-directed action by von Cranach and colleagues at the Psychologisches Institut in the University of Bern, Switzerland.

TAG is a meta-language for defining task languages. It purports to represent the operations and structures that a user may call on to encode information about a language (e.g. a particular dialogue design). It has two levels of description: concepts; and rule schemata. The dictionary of concepts contains the grammatical objects - including what are called "simple tasks", which are tasks the user can perform routinely. The rule-schemata provide mappings from task descriptions to action specifications and capture the syntactic rules of the language (dialogue). It is intended that the TAG model will be developed into a metric which can be applied to dialogue designs in advance of implementation in order to predict the learnability and usability of the designs.

The work by von Cranach and colleagues (e.g. Von Cranach *et al*.,

1982) is concerned with developing a Theory of Concrete Actions. Such actions have the following defining characteristics: They are not laboratory exercises but occur in the real world; they are not routine; they can be completed in one episode; and they are associated with objectively observable behaviour. They are not restricted to user-system interaction but they include this sort of behaviour.

The theory is concerned with the temporal organisation of observable and subjective behaviour into sequences that extend through time, and with the hierarchical organisation of the behaviour into levels. The theory draws heavily on the earlier models of Miller, Galanter and Pribram (1960) and further developments of the Miller et al. work by Hacker (1978). It emphasises the role of feedback in guiding behaviour through a series of hierarchically organised goals, based on repeated comparison of an actual situation with an intended situation.

The theory is divided into the following parts, dealing with:

- course of the action
- organisation levels
- attention processes
- goal determination
- cognitive control
- subconscious self-regulation
- social control
- values and attitudes
- knowledge relevant to the action
- interactive actions.

A strength of the work is the detailed level of its conceptual analysis, and the richness of the accompanying data collection and analysis methods that have been developed. It can be seen from the various parts of the theory listed above that it extends beyond what is normally considered a "cognitive" model in the narrow sense, and it provides a link with the "situational psychological" type of model discussed below.

A number of others are working in this area as well. Riley and O'Malley's (1984) work on planning nets, for example, looks promising, although so far it has been applied only to simple text editing tasks. This approach identifies a series of subgoals that need to be achieved, and for each subgoal identifies the prerequisites, the action the user must take, and the consequences of the action. Norman's (1984) paper discussing four stages of user activities also provides a possible framework for considering design issues. He suggests that in interacting with an electronic system, the user goes through an iterative cycle which involves forming an intention, selecting an appropriate action, executing the action, and evaluating the outcome. For each of these stages he suggests some key aspects of product design which need to be considered. Wells (1984) presents a notational system which is suitable for iterative modelling of specific user-system dialogues, and which allows traditional data flow diagrams to provide a basis for dynamic simulations of user-system interaction suitable for early prototyping. Iivari and Koskela (1984) present their PIOCO methodology, which includes a detailed notational system for describing user-system interaction at several levels in terms of the relationships between the user's work activities and the structure of the information system.

These, and other, attempts to model user-system interaction at a quasi-cognitive level do not all draw on what is known about human cognitive psychology to the same degree. To some extent the onus must be on cognitive psychologists to demonstrate that their science - which purports to provide an understanding of human behaviour - has something useful to say about human behaviour at the interface to an electronic office system. It should also be the case that researchers into user-system interaction should wish to make themselves familiar with relevant research in cognitive psychology.

<u>The situational psychological</u>. A user does not interact with an electronic office system "in a vacuum" but in the context of a total situation. The situation may or may not include other people, or other machines, but it will include more than the very specific observable interactions between the user and the machine that might be the initial focus of interest. It is reasonable to suppose that many of the psychological principles that govern human behaviour in other situations also apply to situations in which the human is interacting with an electronic office system.

This is recognised in the work of von Cranach <u>et al</u>, who include the concepts of situational roles and rules, and other concepts concerned with the social control of action, in their model. Similar concepts appear in the models developed by Argyle and colleagues (e.g. Argyle, Furnham and Graham, 1981).

Argyle <u>et al</u>. propose that situations emerge and have the properties they do because they enable people to attain goals, which in turn are linked to needs and other drives. A similar "evolutionary" concept underlies the discussion of "species of interaction" in the next chapter, where the species of interaction available is one of the most important features defining a situation in which a user interacts with an electronic office system. Species will survive and flourish in the highly competitive office systems marketplace to the extent that they create situations which enable their users to achieve important goals easily.

Sometimes those present in a situation share the same goals, sometimes they do not. In the case of user-system interaction, it is normally important that the electronic system behaves as if it shares the same goals as its user, and not some other set. All the other features of situations can be explained in terms of facilitating the attainment of drive-related goals.

The models developed contain a wide variety of concepts, including, amongst others: steps, and sequences of steps, for attaining goals; rules, for coordinating and constraining behaviour; roles, for division of labour and social control; and others. Situations are conceived of as systems with interdependent parts. Although goals can be considered the natural "independent variables" from which everything else follows, it is also true that a change to any feature of a situation can be expected to cause other features to change as well. This notion of interdependence is also taken up within the psychophysiological context, discussed below.

Murray and Bevan (1984) take the notion that the electronic system should usually behave as if it shares the same goals as its human user further. They argue that human-to-human conversation normally involves social as well as task-oriented goals, and that user-system dialogue should take account of this and mimick the "social aspect" of conversation to an appropriate degree. Consistent with this view, Richards and Underwood (1984) have shown that the social style of communication adopted by the electronic system can influence the social style adopted by the user. For example, subjects in their experiments were more likely to adopt a polite style themselves when the system addressed them with a polite, inexplicit introductory message than when other messages were used. They discuss how effects of this sort could be used to advantage in facilitating speech communication between the user and the system.

<u>Conclusions concerning models of user-system interaction</u>. The examples above illustrate the kind of thing that models of

user-system interaction can address. Such models can be focussed narrowly (e.g. on the physical layout of the keyboard, or the legibility of characters on the screen) or broadly (e.g. describing the whole situation in which the user can be observed to be interacting, or choosing not to interact, with an electronic office system). As the focus broadens, one is likely to need to model what is going on at different levels of description, and in terms of a variety of different constructs which work together in a highly complex system of interdependent parts. This theme is considered further in the following discussion of the psychophysiological context.

THE PSYCHOPHYSIOLOGICAL CONTEXT

The Human User

Psychophysiology recognises that humans working with electronic office systems do not just perform tasks, in the sense of completing them within a particular time period and with a particular level of accuracy or quality. They also respond physiologically (one concern of physical ergonomics, but it goes beyond considerations of the physical ergonomics of the situation), and they have subjective experiences (some, but not all, of which relate directly to the cognitive processes that are the concern of cognitive psychological models of user-system interaction). Psychophysiology is therefore concerned with the whole situation, not just one aspect of it, and in particular, as Gale (1973) has suggested, psychophysiology is concerned with the integration of three domains: overt behaviour; subjective experience; and physiology.

The Human Factors view of user-system interaction needs to take account of the fact that users are humans, and do respond in each of the three domains. The nature of the linkages between these domains can be debated but for practical purposes the Gale and Edwards view (1985) that changes in any one can affect either or both of the other two is probably the safest view to take.

The three can be regarded as three sub-systems within the user of the electronic office system, the user in turn being a component of broader situational, organisational, and societal systems. The sub-systems are all in continuous interaction, their relative dominance within the hierarchy varying according to circumstances. Overlaid on this, people vary in terms of which of their sub-systems tends to be the most dominant in most situations. As recognised by general systems theory, such systems have emergent properties - the whole (of the system) being greater than the sum of its parts (sub-systems).

Emergent Properties of Systems

The fact that systems have important emergent properties means it can be difficult to make predictions about how successful (in terms of user-system interaction) a new electronic office system will be, based only on consideration of one particular aspect of the system in isolation (e.g. time taken to complete a task as a function of the layout of the keyboard). It is necessary to deal with the complexity on its own terms, and not throw it away by dealing with only isolated components.

A practical example is the debate concerning the possible stressful effects of electronic visual displays. An almost universal conclusion drawn by contributors to the volume edited by Grandjean and Vigliani (1982) is that this debate cannot be resolved adequately unless at least all of the following are taken into account:

- the display
- the keyboard
- the whole workstation
- the working environment
- the work organisation
- the task content
- psychosocial aspects
- physiological measures
- subjective variables
- objective performance
- individual differences between different users
- demographic variables

A Need for Ecological Validity

It is proposed below, in discussing the evaluation of office systems, that the complexity that is involved requires a special kind of research environment - an experimental, real-life office - where user-system interaction can be researched in ecologically valid situational and organisational contexts.

The following section considers what the organisational context is. It does not attempt to cover every aspect of an organisation. It focusses on describing the organisational context in terms of the information-processing and communications aspects, which relate most directly to electronic office systems. It will be appreciated from the discussion above that this does not mean that other aspects can be ignored, but it is useful in providing a framework for research that emphasises those aspects of organisations that are most intimately connected to electronic office systems. The other aspects of organisations which affect and are affected by new systems need to be researched, but within the overall information-processing and communications framework. For a broader discussion of organisational aspects of information technology, see Pava (1983).

THE ORGANISATIONAL CONTEXT

A Goal-Need Hierarchy

Extending the notion of a hierarchy of goals that is evident in many models of user-system interaction (see above), and the psychophysiological emphasis on taking account of the higher-level systems within which user-system interaction occurs, this section presents a view of the organisation in terms of a hierarchy of goals, needs, and activities, related to information-processing and communications. It considers these at different levels, working from the highest level downwards, becoming increasingly specific. It considers:

- high level organisational goals
- the functional goals of the managers and professionals whose responsibility it is to translate those high level organizational goals into concrete achievements through the appropriate management of resources
- the information and communication needs which result from the functional goals
- the specific kinds of activities which take place in offices today in order to try and meet the information and communication needs of the organization.

This is the essential functional framework within which opportunities to capitalise on the potential benefits of information technology must be sought. It is only a partial view of organizational reality. By itself it does not take much if any explicit account of the needs of individuals and groups for job satisfaction, for example, or of the informal organization, or of other important aspects of the psychology of organizations. This does not mean that these aspects of organizations can be ignored. Far from it; they need to be taken fully into account in any programme of office automation. Nevertheless, the basic functional view is probably the most appropriate to take as a convenient starting point.

High Level Organizational Goals

New electronic systems will be introduced into organizations only to the extent they are seen to help the organization meet its high level goals. It is important to understand what these broad organizational goals are and how they result in the various more specific needs for communications and the handling of information.

Porter and Roberts (1976), after reviewing the literature, conclude that the following characteristics emerge as being considered by most theorists as essential to the definition of what constitutes an organization. These are summarised here in terms of their implications for organizational communication.

Social composition. Individuals frequently are not only representing themselves when they communicate, they are also serving as agents of an organizational unit. Likewise, even when the apparent recipient of an item is a particular person, the item becomes available potentially to the various units which that person represents. Much communication is, and needs to remain, of a group-to-group nature. Organizations are characterized by people working together in teams, and systems which disrupt this are not likely to be very successful.

Goal orientation. Organizations are ordinarily considered to be purposeful in nature, that they have objectives or goals. This has a decided impact on communication - both within the organization and on the flow of information to and from the environment outside. It influences the pattern of communication networks in terms of the frequency and direction of flow of items, and it influences the content of items. Systems which obscure or detract from this goal orientation are not likely to be very successful. It is essential that new systems take adequate account of the various kinds of goals that characterize different kinds of organizations and different levels within an organization.

Differential functions. This third characteristic of organizations is important in helping them to attain their goals, but inappropriate differentiation can be a hindrance. The parceling out of functions encourages some kinds of interactions and discourages others. A particular implementation may make it very difficult for some patterns to originate or others continue. Differentiation of functions also affects the attitudes of the people involved. This can facilitate communication among those performing similar functions and inhibit it across individuals from different functional areas. New systems need to encourage an appropriate differentiation of functions if they are to be successful.

Systems of coordination. An organization's attempts at rational coordination - e.g. plans, regulations, role prescriptions - are concerned with the coordination of activities, not particular individuals. The coordination of activities requires communication among the parts of the organization, and organizations encourage those sorts of communication that facilitate such integration. Systems which do not facilitate this or, worse, hamper it (e.g. because of difficulties in communicating between one device and another) are not likely to be very successful in terms of this aspect of organizational communication.

Continuity through time. This feature of organizations is one of the key factors distinguishing them from other types of social entities, such as crowds or audiences. It affects communication in organizations because it gives individuals an awareness that their activities and interactions are likely to be repeated (though not precisely identically) in the future. New systems could do well to capitalize on this aspect of organizations by facilitating interaction with the organization's history, e.g. by facilitating the organization and retrieval of information - an area which is very inefficient at present.

Conclusions. Electronic systems must, if they are to be successful, "mesh in" with the organization's "personality" - they must not clash with the fundamental needs of the organization. The chief needs are for:

- social composition
- goal orientation
- differentiation of functions
- coordination of activities
- continuity through time.

Information Needs

The broad organizational goals reviewed above are met by the appropriate management of resources and activities. This inevitably involves information-processing and communications.

Information needs apply at all levels of all divisions in every organisation, from senior management concerned with strategic planning through middle management concerned with managerial control to the operational level concerned with operational control. Figure 2.1 summarises some of the main characteristics of these three organisational levels in relation to their information needs.

At all three levels, the information needs become manifest in the behaviour of the people involved. Whatever technology the people concerned may use - be it paper or electronic - they perform certain basic functions. These include:

- generating information
- storing information
- seeking information
- retrieving information
- using information in a variety of ways
- communicating information to others.

Exactly what the information is depends on the particular organisational division and on the organisational level concerned, as shown in Figure 2.1, but the basic functions involved are common to all divisions and levels and underlie the various specific activities observed in the office environment.

The more specific characteristics of the information needed also vary. Figure 2.2 shows some of the more important differences. Major trends in the business environment are leading to increasing demands on the information requirements of organizations , as shown in Figure 2.3, and this is an important stimulus for organisations to consider using electronic systems.

The emerging electronic technology needs to take account of:

- The information needs of organisations
- The characteristics of information at different organizational levels and in different divisions
- The trends in information requirements shown in Figure 2.3.

The following sections focus on how the broad organizational goals and the information and communications needs that are generated by them are translated by the organization into office

Figure 2.1: Business Information Needs

	Strategic Planning	Managerial Control	Operational Control
Organisational Identity	Corporate general management	Functional management	Supervisors, foremen, clerks
Goals	Set objectives, determine resources	Allocate resources, make rules, measure performance, exert control	Use resources to carry out tasks in conformance with rules
Characteristics	Variable, staff-oriented, external perspective	Judgemental, line-oriented, internal perspective	Logical, predictable, prescribed
Information Inputs	Staff studies, external situation, internal results	Summaries, exceptions	Internal events, transactions
Information Systems	Special reports, enquiries, simulations	Regular reports, enquiries, databanks	Formal, fixed procedures, complex
Information Outputs	Sub-goals, policies, constraints	Decisions, procedures	Actions
Tempo	Irregular	Rhythmic	Real-time

Behaviour (applies to all):
generate information, store information, seek information, retrieve information, use information (in various ways), communicate.

Figure 2.2: Information Characteristics

Strategic	Managerial	Operational
aggregate	more detailed	very detailed
unique	exception	repetitive
predictive	historical/predictive	predictive
within magnitudes	within bounds	very accurate
often non-financial	often financial	often non-financial
wide scope	narrower scope	narrow scope

Figure 2.3: Increasing Demands on Information Systems

Trends In Business Environment	Information Requirements
Faster change	- information must be prompt - information must be oriented towards the future
Increased complexity	- more information is needed - information must be available selectively to avoid swamping management
Larger organisations	- information must generate decisions from the appropriate organisational levels - information must be adaptable to the structural changes in complex organisations - all information presented must have credibility

activities through the work of various types of office workers. The following main categories are distinguished:

- managers and other office principals
- secretaries
- clerical workers.

The information and communications characteristics of the work typically associated with these categories are reviewed below.

FUNCTIONAL ANALYSIS AND DEFINITION OF NEW SERVICES

By "functional analysis" in this context is meant an analysis, within the broad organisational context, of the key functions within an office environment, in terms of their information-processing and communications needs, and the opportunities for new services that can be provided through electronic office systems. Such an analysis is a matter for research, only an outline discussion is presented here.

Management Goals

The manager's role represents a link between the organisation's high level needs reviewed above and the more specific communications and information needs that new technology impacts directly.

Prien and Ronan (1971) after reviewing research findings on job analysis conclude that managerial work can be viewed as consisting of two broad aspects:

- concern for the human element (person oriented)

- impersonal concern for technical plans, programs, and the functions of the organisation (task oriented).

Research on office activities (Short, Williams and Christie, 1976; Christie, 1981) suggests that the first aspect (person oriented) is primarily responsible for meetings and other forms of direct person-person interaction (Type A activities), and the second aspect (task oriented) is primarily responsible for interaction with "papers" and their electronic equivalents (Type B activities).

Prien and Ronan (1971) compare four major factor analytic studies of managerial and executive functions (by Baehr, Hemphill, Prien and Rothe). They identify 15 functions that account for the results of the studies. It is these that electronic systems ultimately must address if they are to serve the fundamental needs of managers. They are listed in Figure 2.4. If electronic office systems aimed at managers do not help managers to perform these key functions then, whatever else they may do, they will not be successful.

Linkage to communication and information activities. Managers communicate and handle information in order to fulfill their role as managers. Unfortunately, there is a dearth of research on the nature of this linkage. This seems to be because the research on the nature of the manager's role has been done largely for application in other areas, such as management selection and training, rather than to further understanding of organisational communications in terms relating to the design of electronic systems. However, some of the things that managers might be expected to do are suggested in Figure 2.5.

Conclusions. To understand the reasons for the kinds of activities that make up a manager's work - e.g. why a manager needs to "allocate and coordinate tasks", or "read and evaluate" - it is necessary to understand the manager's role.

Empirical studies of the manager's role suggest that it can be understood in terms of about 15 main functions which are listed in Figure 2.4. To be successful, new systems aimed at managers must help them to perform one or more of these functions more easily and more effectively than they can using conventional systems.

Other Office Workers

Some of the key aspects of the work of other office workers are indicated in Figure 2.6.

The following sections look in more detail at the kinds of activities that go on in offices to meet an organisation's underlying information needs.

The activities that occur in the office reflect these different aspects of the work, and the higher-level business needs to communicate and handle information. There are two main types of activity, and they apply to all office workers, as follows.

A. People need to interact with other people directly, e.g.

- informal discussions
- more formal meetings
- telephone conversations
- videophone conversations
- audio teleconferences
- audio-video teleconferences

B. People need to interact with a functionally significant store of information. Traditionally this has been paper but increasingly it is an electronic store of some sort. What is stored is information in one form or another, especially:

Figure 2.4: Managerial and executive functions identified by factor analysis as being key aspects of a manager or executive's role. (In arbitrary order.)

1. Setting organisational objectives
2. Improving work procedures
3. Promoting safety
4. Development and technical ideas
5. Judgement and decision-making
6. Developing group cooperation and teamwork
7. Coping with difficulties and emergencies
8. Developing employee potential
9. Supervision of work
10. Self development and improvement
11. Promoting community-organisation relations
12. Handling business reputation
13. Personal demands
14. Manufacturing process administration
15. Union-management relations

Figure 2.5: Some of the activities managers might be expected to do in order to fulfill their higher level functions.

- contacting individual persons (meetings, clients, staff, travel, ...)
- formulation of short individual documents (letters and messages)
- evaluation of reports (reading, condense contents to key issues, evaluation of contents, annotations, investigation of relevant background information)
- generating reports
- preparing presentations
- preparing decisions, taking decisions (formulation of key items to decide on, formulation of decision criteria, evaluation of related background information, simulating consequences, evaluation of consequences, formulate decisions, initiate actions to be taken)
- planning activities of different types (dates - for oneself and others, activities, budgets, ...)
- initiating and controlling activities (communicating basic ideas and constraints, reviewing first results, ...)

Figure 2.6a: Some aspects of an office principal's work

- administration of projects
- definition of working procedures, standards and related regulations
- investigation of relevant regulations from outside
- planning work (dates, ...)
- allocation of staff to individual tasks
- controlling progress (dates, intermediate results)
- retrieving related general and background information
- formulating management reports
- compilation of condensed reports out of others
- administration of staff
- administration of working material
- contacting individual persons (meetings, 'phone, advisory activities, ...)

Figure 2.6b: Some aspects of a secretary's work

- typing individual documents from handwriting, typewriting and dictation
- compiling standardized documents from prefabricated pieces of text according to detailed instructions
- editing individual documents (corrections, modifications, amendments of contents)
- preparing layout of individual documents
- processing mail: distribution of incoming mail, addressing, registration, mailing outgoing items
- processing messages (internal and external), formulation, distribution
- archiving documents (short and medium term)
- compiling proceedings
- administration and distribution of proceedings according to date or event
- keeping different lists, inventories etc. e.g. addresses, phone numbers, office material, ...
- doing calendar services, e.g. registration and management of dates, appointments, ...
- preparing and organizing travel
- preparing internal accounts (e.g. for travel, office material,...)
- assistance activities (switch phone connections, preparing copies, arrange meetings, find people, welcome visitors, ...)
- individual services to persons (preparing coffee, ...)

Figure 2.6c: Some aspects of a clerical worker's work

- receiving and registering externally produced documents (formatted and unformatted)
- adding received documents to relevant file, initialize new proceedings
- extracting information and data from received documents
- examining information and data which belong to the same file in different respects, e.g. completeness, consistency, correctness, ...
- taking decisions according to regulations
- initiating inquiries (external, internal)
- processing inquiries from others
- formulating outgoing messages and standard documents (formatted and unformatted)
- investigating regulations
- archiving documents (short, medium and long term)
- compilation of proceedings
- preparing and archiving protocols of procedure and decisions
- contacting persons (internal meetings, 'phone calls)
- preparing materials, e.g. concepts, studies, designs, technical documents, ...
- compilation of reports
- retrieving background information and knowledge related to specific tasks
- taking various task related decisions
- archiving information and knowledge
- updating archived information and knowledge

- spoken information
- structured data, such as lists
- written text
- graphical information
- static images
- dynamic images

Most information is a combination of these categories. For example, a report is mainly written text but may also contain graphs, images and structured data. Both types of need may become evident during the same episode, e.g. people in meetings often need to refer to papers and to make notes (Type B needs) as well as interacting face to face (Type A). Office technology should take account of this. For example, a teleconferencing system may need to incorporate a high quality audio or audio-video link for direct person-to-person interaction (A) and a facsimile link or VDUs for exchange of papers (B). It follows that a hierarchy of needs and more specific activities reflecting those needs can be defined.

We would not expect specific activities to be related to underlying needs in a very simple way, any more than symptoms of disease are related to particular, underlying disease processes in any simple way. A cough, for example, may be symptomatic of a cold or something more serious. This is why doctors look for patterns of symptoms when deciding on a diagnosis. In a similar way, a telephone call may reflect a need to set up a meeting, a need to confirm a point of fact, a need to obtain some advice quickly, and so on.

In factor-analytic terminology, we can say that specific symptoms, e.g. a cough, "load on" different diseases, e.g. a cold, to varying extents - or, in the present context, specific office activities, e.g. making a telephone call, "load on" different functional needs, e.g. to receive advice urgently, to varying extents.

Factor analysis is a class of mathematical techniques that can be used to describe a set of specific variables (e.g. office activities) in terms of a smaller set of more general factors (e.g. functional needs). It has been applied to the analysis of both Type A and Type B office activities, in the studies covered in the following sections.

Type A needs are those which require direct communication between people in real time. Present technology provides two main ways in which these can be satisfied: face to face meetings of many different sorts, and the telephone. Teleconferencing is a third possibility.

Face to face meetings in business and government have been analysed extensively, but no comparable analysis has been done for telephone calls.

The analysis of face to face meetings was done during the 1970s for the purpose of identifying those types of meetings for which teleconferencing would be suitable. The work is described in some detail by Short, Williams and Christie (1976), and is summarised as follows.

The work began with a series of 65 open-ended interviews, designed to elicit words and phrases that managers and professionals found natural to describe their meetings. The informants were drawn from a range of different offices in Greater London. A questionnaire was then developed which asked respondents to describe a single recent meeting in detail, in terms of 104 rating scales based on the results of the earlier interviews. This questionnaire was completed by 311 managers and professionals in various business organisations.

Factor analysis of the questionnaire returns was used to define nine orthogonal factors which accounted for most of the differences between the meetings described by the respondents. The nine factors are listed in Figure 2.7. It must be stressed that the factors do not represent the totality of managers' and professionals' work by any means, but in various combinations they do provide a fairly good way of describing the underlying functional needs served by most of the meetings held in the sample studied. The analysis was used as one input in assessing the potential for teleconferencing services.

Type B needs are those which require people to interact with information rather than directly with other people. In offices today this normally involves paper, but increasingly it involves information in electronic form.

Christie (1981) reports an analysis of Type B needs done for the Commission of the European Communities to provide one input into its long range planning for new electronic information services. The analysis was based on 225 questionnaires completed by officials in various parts of the Commission's offices in Brussels and Luxembourg.

Factor analysis of the 41 questionnaire items identified six main Type B factors, listed in Figure 2.8.

The needs identified above form a broad framework in which specific activities are carried out to meet those needs. Understanding what specific activities go on in the office can help in the design of systems to support users' needs.

Figure 2.9 presents a breakdown of office activities based on a survey by Engel _et al_. (1979) in a multinational corporation. Clear examples of Type A and Type B activities have been identified as such. The activities in the "other" category also relate to these two main categories but less clearly. It should be noted that whilst the Engel _et al_. study is illustrative of

Figure 2.7: Type A needs identified by factor analysis, as being among the more important reasons for holding meetings. (In arbitary order.)

1. Need to allocate and coordinate tasks

2. Need to give and/or receive information

3. Need to maintain discipline

4. Need to present and/or discuss a report

5. Need to discuss a problem

6. Need to appraise another party's services or products

7. Need to review subordinates' work

8. Need to make tactical or policy decisions

9. Need to provide advice

Figure 2.8: Type B needs identified by factor analysis as being among the more important reasons for using a paper-based or electronic information service. (In arbitrary order.)

1. Need to read and evaluate

2. Need to provide information

3. Need to complete forms (for administrative or other purposes)

4. Need to access local files (e.g. personal and divisional)

5. Need to access remote files (e.g. computerised systems and other services widely available to many people)

6. Need to access non-personal but specialist files (e.g. the 'document centres' in the Commission)

Figure 2.9a: Breakdown of office activities (principals)[+]

Activities	Average percent of time			
	Level 1	Level 2	Level 3	All
Type A Communication	38.2	26.8	19.5	26.5
. telephone	13.8	12.3	11.3	12.3
. conferring with secretary	2.9	2.1	1.0	1.8
. scheduled meetings	13.1	6.7	3.8	7.0
. unscheduled meetings	8.5	5.7	3.4	5.4
Type B Communication	38.3	47.4	44.2	44.2
. writing	9.8	17.2	17.8	15.6
. proofreading	1.8	2.5	2.4	2.3
. searching	3.0	6.4	6.4	5.6
. reading	8.7	7.4	6.3	7.3
. filing	1.1	2.0	2.5	2.0
. retrieving filed information	1.8	3.7	4.3	3.6
. dictating to secretary	4.9	1.7	0.4	1.9
. dictating to a machine	1.0	0.9	0.0	0.6
. copying	.1	.6	1.4	.9
. mail handling	6.1	5.0	2.7	4.4
Other	23.3	25.9	36.0	29.4
. calculating	2.3	5.8	9.6	6.6
. planning or scheduling	4.7	5.5	2.9	4.3
. travelling outside HQ	13.1	6.6	2.2	6.4
. using equipment	.1	1.3	9.9	4.4
. other	3.1	6.7	11.4	7.7
	100%	100%	100%	100%
total number of principals	76	123	130	329

Level 1 = upper management
Level 2 = other management
Level 3 = nonmanagement

[+]See footnote on page 57.

Figure 2.9b: Breakdown of office activities (secretaries)[+]

Activities	Average percent of time
Type A Communication	14.8
. telephone	10.5
. conferring with principals	4.3
Type B Communication	79.9
. writing	3.5
. mail handling	8.1
. bulk envelope stuffing	1.4
. collating/sorting	2.6
. proofreading	3.9
. reading	1.7
. typing	37.0
. copying or duplication	6.2
. taking shorthand	5.5
. filing	4.6
. pulling files	2.8
. keeping calendars	2.6
Other	5.5
. pick-up or delivery	2.2
. using equipment	1.3
. other	2.0
	100%
total number of secretaries	123

[+]See footnote on page 57.

Figure 2.9c: Breakdown of office activities (clerical workers)[+]

Activities	Average percent of time
Type A Communication	**11.1**
. telephone	9.2
. meetings	1.9
Type B Communication	**68.2**
. filling out forms	8.3
. writing	7.3
. typing	7.8
. collating/sorting	5.2
. checking documents	10.5
. reading	2.9
. filing	5.9
. looking for information	10.2
. copying or duplication	3.9
. using a terminal	6.3
Other	**20.7**
. calculating	10.3
. pick-up or delivery in HQ	.8
. scheduling or dispatching	1.2
. other	8.4
	100%
total number of clerical workers	115

the various surveys that have been done, the results of different studies have varied somewhat. Doswell (1983) compares the findings from several of the main studies that have been done. No representative sample survey of office activities based on adequate methodology suitable for drawing generalizable conclusions has yet been published.

The sort of breakdown achieved in Figure 2.9 is useful for indicating the variety of activities involved and - to the extent the findings are reliable - how relatively time-consuming they tend to be in the traditional office.

Much more detailed analysis - taking account of the structure, interrelationships and functional significance of the activities - is required to provide a basis for adequate inputs to the technology design process, and this is an important aspect of modern human factors research in this area.

Both types of activity are essential but Type B tend to be the more time-consuming in the office. This is a major justification for the rapid development of technology in this area in recent years. It also reflects an increasing user awareness of needs in this area. Word processors, electronic mail, electronic storage and retrieval, and other type B systems have taken off in a way unparalleled by audio conferencing, audio-video conferencing and other Type A systems apart from the extraordinarily successful voice telephone. The emphasis of current Human Factors research is on Type B needs and systems to reflect the current and increasing level of interest in this area of technology.

Based on the Engel _et al_. study, it would seem that about 43% of the time managers and professionals spend on Type B activities (or 20% of total time - the equivalent of one whole day a week) is spent on relatively non-productive Type B activities (eg. filing, as opposed to reading and writing). Details are given in Figure 2.10.

Figure 2.10: Managers' and professionals' productive and non-productive Type B activities.

	% of Type B	% of Total Time
'Productive'	57.5	25.4
. writing	35.3	15.6
. dictating to secretary	4.3	1.9
. dictating to a machine	1.4	0.6
. reading	16.5	7.3
'Non-productive'	42.5	18.8
. proofreading	5.2	2.3
. searching	12.7	5.6
. filing	4.5	2.0
. retrieving filed information	8.1	3.6
. copying	2.0	0.9
. mail handling	9.9	4.4

Types of Information

It is important to distinguish between different types of information in considering Type B needs and systems because they have technological as well as psychological significance. A picture may often be "worth a thousand words" in psychological terms but it also has different, more demanding technological requirements.

The broad distinction between text, graphics and images is especially important. Text can be stored efficiently in electronic form by encoding each character. Graphical information can often be stored in a reduced form as well, e.g. by specifying the start and end points of a series of lines, but often requires a significantly higher-resolution display than does text. Image information is even more demanding. A document image is formed by scanning the document and storing a very detailed dot-matrix type representation of it, much like a television picture. The quality of the image improves as the number of dots increases, requiring a very large amount of information to be processed and stored by the system.

The storage of a memorandum or letter illustrates the difference between text and image information. A memorandum produced internally could be typed into an electronic mail system which could process and store it in coded form with minimal requirements on storage and with the possibility of transmitting the item speedily over a relatively narrowband channel such as a standard telephone line. A letter received from outside (i.e. typed on paper) could also be put into the system, but not so easily. It could be retyped, but this is time-consuming. It could be fed throughout an optical character recognition machine which would recognise the individual letters and code them, but suffers from several weaknesses (e.g. probable inability to code the letter heading, and failure to code the signature).

Alternatively it could be scanned to produce an image (facsimile), but this also has some disadvantages (e.g. the storage requirement varies with the type of system but may be very high, transmission rate over relatively narrowband channels may be slow, and the information cannot be word processed as it can if it is coded). Typically, the amount of electronic storage for an image of a page of text is fifty times more than for the same text coded, although this can be reduced using special techniques.

Main Functions

To understand the roles that new technology can play in the office, it is necessary to consider not only the type of information involved but also what users need to do with it. The various specific activities (e.g. typing, word processing) that might be involved are related to the following main functions:

- production of items (e.g. dictating, typing, word processing)
- storage of items (e.g. classification, indexing)
- retrieval of items (e.g. from personal files, current record libraries, archives)
- use of items (e.g. to incorporate in standard letters, to support decision-making, to produce an updated version of a report, etc.)
- distribution of items. (e.g. one-to-one, such as a letter; one-to-many, such as a memorandum; and many-to-one, such as collection of questionnaire returns).

Figure 2.11 summarises the main functions in terms of the two main types of activity and the main types of information involved. Examples are given to illustrate various kinds of technology within this framework of user needs. Figure 2.11 is merely illustrative, however, and the examples are just examples. The situation is more complicated than the figure might suggest - for example, microfiche can also be used to store text and data as well as image information.

Technologically, the various elements in Figure 2.11 are being increasingly bound together in two important ways:

- an underlying trend to represent all different forms of information in a single, common, basic representation: in digital form

- a gradual development of standards (of codes and procedures) for exchange of information.

Both of these trends help to meet a general user need to be able to work with a variety of different types of information flexibly within a common technology (once paper, now electronic systems).

EVALUATION OF SYSTEMS

The preceeding sections have described the context for which electronic office systems need to be developed, and in terms of which they need to be evaluated. The view advocated here is that electronic office systems need to be evaluated in terms of how well they address the total problem as described above, not just one particular aspect of it.

Evaluation therefore needs to address:

Figure 2.11: Elements of information-communication activities in the office.

Activity	Type of Information: Voice	Data	Text	Image
Type A formal, informal, person-to-person, group-to-group, etc.	telephone, audio tele-conference			video-, phone, audio-video tele-conf.
Type B production, e.g. of: . letter . report . contract	dictation, store-and-forward voice, speech recognition		word processing	
Information seeking, storage and retrieval: . personal files . current records . archives . external information . etc.		computer	scientific and technical information databases, shared-logic word processing, optical character readers, videotex	micro-fiche, micro-film, video-disc, optical disc
use: . incorporation . decision-making . influencing confidence . citation . to inform . etc.		computer models	word processing	photo-copying 'cut and paste'
communication: . one-to-one . one-to-many . many-to-one	telecon-ference	computer systems	videotex, electronic mail, communicating word processors, computer conferencing	facs-simile

- the behavioural, cognitive, affective and physiological aspects of user-system interaction, identified and defined within the psychophysiological framework - this depends upon adequate models of user-system interaction being developed, in order to be able to define the appropriate measures for evaluation

- the organisational context, including individual and group effectiveness in contributing to the achievement of organisational goals, as well as socio-economic factors relating to the individual, the work group, and the wider context - this depends upon an adequate definition and specification of the high-level services to be provided, and their lower-level components.

A fundamental requirement is the development of an overall methodology - a complete structural and procedural research environment - that is optimal for researching new electronic office systems. The need for such a methodology comes from the need to deal with the complexity of the problem on its own terms, rather than solving simpler problems that are more amenable to control and quantification but which do not contribute as fully to the development of new and better concepts in electronic office systems.

Traditional Human Factors methods need to be developed further in order to achieve this aim. The technology of electronic office systems is evolving so rapidly that it is outstripping our understanding of the human aspects, and Human Factors needs to adapt to this situation and develop new and more appropriate methods of research.

CAFE OF EVE. Consistent with the promise of a knowledge explosion that is associated with the development of new electronic systems, and the emphasis within Human Factors on the human aspects of this, the term CAFE OF EVE has been proposed for the new methodology that is required (Gale and colleagues, Southampton University). The CAFE OF EVE would be a Controlled, Adaptive, Flexible, Experimental Office of the Future, in an Ecologically Valid Environment. It would combine the most appropriate features of controlled laboratory experimental methods with the most appropriate features of field research methods, and add some new, emergent properties.

The CAFE OF EVE would provide an environment in which evaluation of electronic office systems could be conducted at all levels, and at all stages of the design process. It would therefore provide a total answer to the problem, and not just a partial answer to some particular aspect of it. In addition, it would provide a European Showcase in which new and effective concepts in electronic office systems could be demonstrated in a real working environment.

The concept of the CAFE OF EVE is explained further in Chapter 6, as a key area for research.

AREAS WHERE RESEARCH IS NEEDED

Research on what people in offices do and will need to do in an electronic environment is needed in order to:

- segment the population of potential users of office systems according to their needs, and to define the main categories of office systems that will be required in order to meet those needs

- identify the key services which office systems in each major category need to provide.

A Language for Describing Office Information Processing

A necessary prerequisite to systematic research is a scheme for describing the information processing that electronic office systems are meant to address. A number of approaches to this have been discussed in the literature (e.g. Ellis, 1979; Hammer and Kunin, 1980; Lebensold, Radhakrishnan and Jaworski, 1982; Nutt and Ricci, 1981; Van de Ven and Ferry, 1980). These need to be reviewed as a basis for developing a language suitable for describing the organisational information processing context in which user-system interaction occurs. The language needs to be capable of forming a conceptual link between high-level organisational concepts relating to organisational goals, information needs, and so forth, and the more detailed models that deal with user-system interaction at a situational/cognitive level.

Segmenting the User Population

The need here is to define the different categories of office workers to whom electronic systems will be offered. The categories need to be defined in terms that relate directly to the kinds of things the people concerned will need to do with the systems. This means that one needs to take account of changes that the movement towards an electronic environment can be expected to bring about. The kinds of things that a manager, a scientific professional, a secretary, and a clerical worker will do in an electronic office environment can be expected to be different from what they do in the paper-based environment of today, and consequently the traditional way of categorizing office workers (e.g. manager, secretary, etc.) may not be as useful as some new scheme that cuts across the traditional distinctions. (The language referred to above for describing office information processing needs to ba capable of handling these sorts of changes.)

The changes will reflect different, and better, ways of addressing the same underlying organizational and human needs. This statement itself may only be approximately true. It is conceivable that organizational and personal goals will themselves change, but the major changes in the next five to ten years are likely to be largely in terms of addressing the same goals in better ways.

The segmentation of the population of potential users therefore needs to be based on a thorough, scientific analysis and survey of organizational goals and sub-goals, covering a representative sample of different organizations. Where it is possible to obtain indications of probable changes in organizational goals and sub-goals over the next five to ten years, these should be included.

This analysis of the organisation needs to be complemented by an analysis of how the various goals and sub-goals depend upon and/or generate information/communications. Consideration needs to be given to which of the various information- and communication-related activities that are identified could be allocated to electronic systems and which would be done by humans.

Once it has been decided which functions would best be allocated to the humans in the electronic office environment it should be possible to define a set of categories, according to the functions involved, that define the major types of user of electronic office systems. These categories would define the major set of roles that can be expected for humans in the office of the next five to ten years. In some ways they may approximate the traditional roles of manager, secretary, etc., but in many ways they will probably be different. (For example, even today the ready availability of word processing has meant that more and more managers and professionals are addressing the low-level goal of document-creation by themselves with little or no involvement of a secretary or typist.)

Some quantification and forecasting should be possible in terms of the numbers of users falling into the various categories defined so long as the survey of organisational functions in terms of goals and sub-goals is done appropriately (e.g. based on a representative sample, and using adequate data collection and analysis techniques).

Identifying Key Services

The allocation of functions between electronic systems and humans should lead directly to an identification of the key services which the electronic systems will need to provide. In some ways they may correspond to services which are defined by simple extrapolation from the paper-based environment (e.g. word processing instead of typing, electronic mail instead of paper-based mail) but they may also include other, new kinds of services that become apparent once one looks at the goals and sub-goals involved (what people are trying to achieve) rather than simply the directly observable aspects of their work.

Research on Models of User-System Interaction

Developing appropriate models of user-system interaction is needed as a basis for developing appropriate ways of implementing new services identified, and for evaluating new systems. The models need to be developed at different levels. They need to recognise that the user is a psychophysiological, not *just* cognitive, system. They also need to recognise that the human is just one sub-system within the total human-machine system, and that the machine also needs to be incorporated into the models.

There is therefore a need to draw on psychology, artificial intelligence, and possibly other disciplines, to develop a new kind of model that is suitable for modelling the hybrid, electronic/biological/psychological system that is the subject-matter of user-system interaction.

Research on Evaluation

A new methodology needs to be developed that goes beyond traditional Human Factors methods. This new methodology, the CAFE OF EVE, is discussed further in Chapter 6.

SUGGESTED FURTHER READING

Argyle, M., Furnham, A., & Graham, J.A. (1981)
Social situations. Cambridge: Cambridge University Press.

Birchall, D.W. and Hammond, V.J. (1981)
Tommorrow's office today: managing technological change. London: Business Books, Hutchinson Publishing Group.

Cakir, A., Hart, D.J., & Stewart, T.M.F. (1980)
Visual display terminals: a manual covering ergonomics, workplace design, health and safety and task organisation. Chichester: John Wiley & Sons.

Card, S.K., Moran, T.P., & Newell, A. (1983)
The psychology of human-computer interaction. London/New Jersey: Lawrence Erlbaum Associates.

Cranach, M. von, Kalbermatten, U., Indermuhle, K., and Gugler, B. (1982)
Goal-directed action. London: Academic Press.

Doswell, A. (1983)
Office automation. Chichester: John Wiley & Sons.

Grandjean, E. & Vigliani, E. (1982) (eds.)
Ergonomic aspects of visual display terminals. London: Taylor and Francis.

Otway, H.J. & Peltu, M. (1983)
New office technology: human and organizational aspects, A publication from the INSIS (Inter-institutional Integrated Services Information System) Programme of the Commission of the European Communities. London: Frances Pinter for the Commission of the European Communities.

Pava, C. (1983)
Managing new office technology: an organizational strategy. London: Collier Macmillan.

THE NEXT CHAPTER

Having described the problem at large, we focus our attention in the next chapter on the specific flows of information across the physical user-system interface, and consider the ever-increasing range of input-output technologies that are opening up more and more possibilities for the interaction between human and machine. The kinds of interactions concerned will form the building blocks of the kinds of activities that will make up office work in the electronic environment.

CHAPTER 3:

SPECIES OF INTERACTION

INTRODUCTION

This chapter focusses on the technology of information input and output. The approach taken recognises that when one observes any user-system interaction one is observing a complex system in which task, technology and human subsystems interact to produce the observable result. Accordingly, it would be a mistake to try and consider input devices in isolation, or output devices in isolation. One needs a way of discussing them that recognises their functional interrelatedness when they are used to perform tasks.

The concept used to meet this requirement is "species of interaction". An analogy is seen with the evolution of the biological species which have developed as an adaptation to their environment. So too we can consider species of input-output interaction similarly to be evolving as an adaptation to the electronic office environment.

The chapter is organised around the main "species", describing their characteristics in terms of the input method, output method and the interaction method used. This does not mean that the characteristics of any given "species" are unique to that "species". One must also recognise that many variants on a given "species" are possible. The aim here is not to be comprehensive but rather to illustrate what is typical within each main "species". The "species" selected for review are:

- Keying - seeing
- Selecting - seeing
- Touching - seeing
- Speaking - hearing
- Looking - seeing
- Gesturing
- Multimedia interaction.

KEYING-SEEING

Keying input through a keyboard and seeing the output from a visual display unit (VDU) is the dominant form of user interface to a computer system; this is true whether the users be experienced or naive and whether the task is simple or complex.

As a consequence a great deal of research has been done into the design of these components with respect to their impact on the user; much of this work has been with the physical characteristics of users in mind and is expressed in ergonomics data.

Input Requirements - Keying

Keying provides an extremely flexible way of entering data; each key is equivalent to the basic unit of human communication which can be formed lexically, syntactically, and semantically into complex communications. However the burden of keying input rests with the user, the system providing little real support. It can be considered the lowest common denominator for communication between human and machine, eliminating problems arising from illegibility in handwriting to provide a standardised form of expression.

The human factors of keying can be considered in terms of the alpha keys, the numeric keys, the function keys, and the ergonomics of the overall design of the keyboard.

The alpha keys. The layout of the alpha keys needs to be considered in relation to the different needs of experienced and inexperienced users.

In the case of experienced users the concern is primarily with the speed of keying. The Qwerty layout is the dominant form for typewriters and has become the standard for all keyboards. Alternative designs have been proposed - such as the Dvorak layout - and these can often facilitate faster typing (typically a five to ten per cent improvement) but the Qwerty layout has become so dominant over the decades that there would seem to be little prospect of alternatives becoming very popular in the foreseeable future.

The Qwerty layout is a disadvantage in cases where keyboard size is important - for example in aircraft cockpits or in portable equipment - and there may be a case for alternative layouts in such circumstances.

Numeric keys. It is generally recommended that a numeric keypad be provided that is separate from the alpha keys. For most purposes both the telephone style layout of keys and the calculator style are equally efficient.

Function keys. These are keys on the keyboard which can be programmed by software to perform particular standard functions (e.g. in word processing such functions might include "cut" and "paste"). They can be "hard function keys", in which case they always perform the same functions; "soft function keys", in which case their function varies according to circumstances; or "user-defined function keys", which are soft function keys that the user can programme to perform chosen functions.

Keyboard design ergonomics. The operation of the keyboard requires a specific working posture; the minimum requirement to achieve this is that the keyboard be detached from the VDU in order that the user can adjust it to achieve greatest comfort. Other important requirements concern the height, profile, and angle of the keyboard since these affect the position and motion of the hands and fingers while keying. Whilst there are recommended ranges for each of these variables, users should normally be able to adjust them to their own needs.

Output Requirements - Seeing

The cathode ray tube or CRT is the basic element around which the display terminals in this group are constructed. The dominant technology in use to provide low cost displays is the refreshed CRT in which the image must be continually refreshed in order to maintain a stable image to the user; this technology is typically found in the domestic television set.

The ability to see an object in a visual display unit (VDU) is chiefly dependent on the eyesight of the individual, the characteristics of the device, the legibility of the displayed items, and the ambient environment.

Legibility of the displayed items. Legibility is defined as the ability to detect and discriminate between individual characters in a displayed group; character size is one of the components contributing to the visual quality of the display. This ability to detect and recognise characters is related to the visual acuity of the user which represents the resolving power of the eye and determines the smallest size we can see. The visual quality of the display is determined by the interaction between the electron beam and the screen phosphor, the method of character generation and the impact of environmental factors. These parameters affecting the user and the display are well understood through ergonomic studies and are implemented in varying degrees by manufacturers.

Environmental Factors. The principal factor affecting the display is glare caused either directly from the VDU by high luminance levels, or indirectly by reflections from windows, light fixtures and other sources of light. Many methods are available for treating reflected glare including etching the surface of the VDU glass, and using filters; all of these methods are reported to be preferable to untreated surfaces. Direct glare can be alleviated by a user variable control to modify the luminance of the VDU.

Alternatives to Keying-Seeing

A significant disadvantage of using a keyboard for many new users of office systems is the need to learn how to type. It would be helpful if the electronic system could offer the user the option of handwriting material as a means of input, instead of keying. Some systems have appeared on the market which allow the user to handwrite material using block capitals, but this can be a little unnatural in many circumstances. Higgins and Whitrow (1984) have proposed a method for recognising cursive script, which would be a more natural alternative.

It should also be recognised that it is not always necessary for the system to recognise the words that have been entered. Entries into an electronic diary or notebook, for example, could be done in graphics - a stored image of the user's handwritten notes without the need for the machine to recognise the words. The same applies to some other applications, such as informal notes sent from one person to another through an electronic system, where neatness and the ability to edit the text (except in limited ways, using graphics manipulation techniques) may not be important.

Even if the user is a skilled typist, conventional keying can be a relatively slow process in some circumstances, such as when a verbatim account of proceedings in needed. Downton and Brooks (1984) and Dye, Newell and Arnott (1984) have outlined methods of machine shorthand transcription based on Palantype (the U.S. equivalent being Stenographic input), and Leedham, Downton, Brooks and Newell (1984) have discussed how Pitman's handwritten shorthand could provide a basis for rapid input to an electronic system.

Where significant editing of text is required, as in typical word processing situations, there arises the need to locate offending characters and replace them. This is usually done using cursor keys or a mouse. Haller, Mutschler and Voss (1984) have compared different possibilities experimentally. They compared the light pen, graphic tablet, mouse, tracking ball (bowling ball or cat), cursor keys and speech recogniser for positioning the cursor over the erroneous character. Speed of performance corresponded roughly to the degree of compatibility between the positioning method used and the system's response, with speech input as the slowest and light pen as the fastest. After the erroneous character had been located, it was necessary to replace it with the correct character. No difference was observed between the two possibilities compared, keying in the correct character or speaking it.

SELECTING-SEEING

The most common method of interaction within this class uses a keyboard for input, a VDU for output, and a menu from which the user can select the appropriate option. This environment is ideal for inexperienced users since they are guided through each stage of the interaction by an appropriate set of menu options presented as a list.

The principal means of indicating the item to be selected from a menu on a VDU screen is the cursor. This is movable and allows the user to indicate the desired display options. Cursor designs typically include a number of features such as a distinctive visual form in terms of shape or blink characteristics. The cursor remains in position until moved by the user with the selection device or moved by the system in response to some user action.

Alongside the development of the selection devices, there have been developments in display technology to produce increasingly high resolution. This has led to the development of graphics displays and complementary interaction methods to enable the manipulation of graphics images.

Input Requirements - Selecting

A number of technologies have developed to ease the way in which the selection of an option is indicated to the system by the user. Three groups can be distinguished, in which

- cursor movements are discrete
- cursor movements are continuous
- actions are direct.

Discrete cursor movement. Discrete cursor movement time is directly proportional to the number of user key strokes. There are two main devices in this class, step keys and text keys. Step keys are typically located on the keyboard in a five key cluster. Keys to move the cursor in each of four directions one character at a time surround a central home key; the home key causes cursor movement to a designated home position, usually the upper left corner of the screen. Text keys are a form of function key usually found on the keyboards of commercial word processors. Each of the keys has a system designated function associated with cursor movement and indicated by a legend on the key top.

Continuous Cursor Movement. There are three main devices in this class: the joystick, cat (or bowling ball) and the mouse. A joystick is a two dimensional control constructed typically as a small strain gauge on which is mounted a rubber knob. Applying force to the joystick in any direction causes the cursor to move in the appropriate direction. (Simpler joysticks used for some computer games simply operate a set of switches.) A cat is a two-dimensional controller resting on two multiturn potentiometers placed at right angles to each other. Turning the ball moves the potentiometers which in turn moves the cursor. A mouse is similar to a cat in so far as it consists of a small bearing the movements of which transmit x-y coordinates in a similar way to the cat, but the bearing is mounted in a small hand-held device which is movable over the desktop; as the mouse moves, a cursor moves simultaneously on the screen. Both the joystick and the mouse may include buttons which the user can press in order to transmit additional signals to the VDU; for example, once the mouse is positioned on target a switch set into the head of the mouse is depressed to indicate selection.

Direct Action. There are two main devices in this class: the lightpen and the digitiser tablet. A lightpen is a device which senses light emitted from the screen. The selector pen emits light and its location is sensed by the light within the VDU. It is not strictly a selection device as it is more normally used for drawing. A digitiser tablet is typically a copper screen, flat on the worksurface on which the user uses a stylus. Electrical connections embedded in the screen control cursor movement. Again it is not strictly a selection device but is used to input data for image manipulation.

Device comparisons. The human factors of selecting can be considered from the point of view of the criteria to be used in choosing a selection device. These include how long it takes users to learn how to use the device, the rate of performance improvement over time, the speed of cursor movement, and how precisely the user can position the cursor at the desired location on the screen.

An important factor influencing accuracy is the ratio of control movement to display movement. When the ratio is small, (generally less than 1.0, as in the case of the joystick), a very small control movement will produce a large cursor movement; this increases the speed of cursor movement, but reduces accuracy, and fine adjustment movements may be necessary. When the ratio is large (generally 1.0 or greater, as in the case of step keys), speed suffers but the user can place the cursor with a much higher degree of accuracy.

In comparative tests, the mouse has often come out quite well (e.g. Card, English and Burr, 1978). Compared with step keys, text keys, and joystick, the mouse is amongst the easiest to learn and normally shows performance improvement over time; it can be the fastest and most accurate device to use for positioning a cursor on a screen. However, this is not always the case. Karat, McDonald and Anderson (1984), for example, showed an advantage for on-screen touch panel over keyboard selection, and for keyboard over mouse. They discuss possible reasons for the difference between their results and previous findings in terms of a variety of factors including type of task, level of user skill, differential familiarity with the devices, and other factors. They also note slightly different results for their performance criteria and for their preference data (their subjects expressing a preference for the keyboard in circumstances where their performance was better with the touch screen).

Differences between performance data and preference data are not unusual. For example, Francas, Goodman and Dickinson (1984) found that subjects trained to a high standard of proficiency in using the Telidon videotex system preferred a full-sized keyboard for input even though it did not lead to improved performance compared with a minimal-function keypad.

The complexity of what is involved, in terms of the variety of factors that can affect which device is best, and differences between different measurement criteria (e.g. performance compared with users' preferences) may be unfortunate for the product designer, but from the psychophysiological perspective introduced in chapter 2 it should come as no surprise.

Output Requirements - Seeing

The bit mapped display is the basic element around which the display terminals in this group are constructed. A bit mapped display is able to address individually each dot or picture element (known as a pixel) making up the display screen. Bit map displays require at least one bit of memory for every pixel on the screen to produce a black and white image; additional bits are required to support grey level and colour images. As a result high resolution displays are more expensive than alphanumeric displays.

The power of a bit-mapped display is in its ability to use high resolution to produce complex graphic images. These can be used to maintain fidelity of reproduction with real-world counterparts, and to support the use of new elements in dialogue design, including the use of icons and of windows.

Icons. Icons are graphical respresentations of real-world artefacts encoded in a symbolic form. They can be used to represent a wide range of objects such as pages of text, books, documents and files. The supporting software can cause the icon to assume some of the properties of its real-world counterpart. They may be arranged on the high resolution display in two dimensional information spaces. The technique of organising and accessing information represented by icons in a two dimensional framework is known as "spatial data management" and any system using such techniques is known as a "spatial data management system". The essence of such a system is in accessing an item by location rather than by name.

Windows. Windows can be defined as partitions of variable size and position in a high resolution display. They enable multiple views of one or more process operations to be maintained in an interactive system; in this way the user can activate a number of tasks and switch contexts between the windows representing the tasks. Windows have been used in several systems to display text (for example, multiple documents), line drawings and graphic images. Systems supporting windows typically feature rapid refresh rates for window movement and update, the automatic reduction of window size while the associated process is inactive and the maintenance of information concerning the state of window processes.

The combination of the mouse selection device and graphics display has produced a new kind of product in the office workstation. One such product is the Lisa "personal office system", and more recently the Macintosh, both developed by Apple Computer Inc., USA. Various other packages in a similar vein (e.g. GEM) are also now appearing on the market.

Lisa, an acronym for Local Integrated Software Architecture, is designed to minimise the use of a keyboard. Lisa consists of a high resolution black and white bit mapped graphics display which is used to provide a facsimile of the office user's desktop. As such, icons are used to represent familiar office objects such as files, pads of paper, wastebasket, and a clipboard which may be used for the temporary storage of portions of documents. Other icons are used to represent a clock, calculator, and various Lisa peripherals such as the disks and printer. Icons may be named objects in order to distinguish instances of the same object type. Icons are selected using a mouse to position an arrow-shaped cursor within the desired object and then pressing the mouse selection button; feedback is provided by an audible click and by the item selected being displayed in reverse video. Objects are deleted by selecting them and then moving them to the icon representing a wastebasket.

Although many of the functions in the Lisa are displayed as icons, commands are used to describe the actions which can be performed with the functions. These commands are displayed as groups in a 'menu bar' at the top of the VDU screen with only those relevant to the user's current context being on display at any given time. A command is selected using the mouse which causes a menu list to be displayed of all commands relevant to that group; each of these can then be selected using the mouse. One such command is known as the "open" command; selection of an icon followed by the "open" command causes the selected object to be projected as a rectangular window displaying the object's contents.

The windows have a standard organisation. At the top they contain an icon of the object and its name. Along their right side and at the bottom of the window are scrolling controls, again in iconic form; these enable the window to be rotated in a vertical or horizontal direction. The window can be adjusted in size either to increase the amount of information visible or to reduce it appropriately; similarly the window may be moved in its entirety around the face of the display.

Multiple windows can be on display simultaneously and they may overlap; in this manner they convey the impression of a file of documents on the user's desk, of which the one currently active is the one that is visible to the user. This impression is enhanced by the fact that only the contents of the active window are completely visible and only its name is shown. Making another window active is achieved by selecting it with the mouse; as a consequence it then assumes the position on the top of the pile of documents. Operations in the window are achieved by moving the appropriate icon with the mouse into the window and using the command to open it.

In this way Lisa provides a common user environment to a number of built-in applications of which seven are initially provided. These are: LisaCalc, providing a spreadsheet system for financial planning; LisaWrite, for text processing; LisaGraph, for creating business graphics such as tables and bar charts; LisaDraw, for preparing drawings and diagrams; LisaProject, for planning projects; LisaList, for creating and editing lists; and LisaTerminal, for networking.

It can be seen that this approach avoides requiring the user explicitly to load a software program; the software is loaded implicitly through associating the appropriate icon with the object. For example, the icon representing a spreadsheet as a sheet of paper with horizontal and vertical lines is automatically processed by LisaCalc when selected; similarly the icon representing a scheduling document as a sheet of paper with interconnecting tasks and milestones is automatically processed by LisaProject. A further example can be seen in the icon representing a written document as a sheet with scribbled text which is automatically processed by LisaWrite; text can be shown in any of eleven type faces and type sizes and in addition can be enhanced using underlined, italic, superscript and subscript versions of each type face. One of the particular advantages of high resolution graphics displays is that documents can be formatted with accurate fidelity to their final printed form, that is, "what you see is what you get" (sometimes referred to as "WYSIWYG").

The printers available with Lisa give the option of producing graphics output and typewriter-like output. A Qwerty format keyboard is provided with the Lisa for keying text; it includes a separate numeric keypad with embedded step keys which are principally used for small movements of the cursor between the cells of spreadsheets. A number of additional keys are provided to enable frequently-used commands as an alternative to selection from the display using the mouse.

The use of icons representing familiar office objects and incorporated into a spatial representation of the user's office desktop presents a familiar environment to the office user. Add to this an integrated set of office "tools" which allow the user to perform tasks using office terminology avoiding computer jargon then an interface is provided which begins to meet the needs of the inexperienced user. Whilst this is clearly a step forward, it is clear that the power of the new technology in the longer term could transform the functions performed in the office and the roles of the users in ways that go beyond the model of the office incorporated in the current Lisa approach.

TOUCHING-SEEING

Touching what we see is one of our most basic forms of communication; it provides a natural and direct means of indicating selection and choice and is the means by which we operate many of the mechanisms available to us through switches, knobs and other forms of control. Technologies have been developed to detect touch and these are combined with display devices to provide a mode of interaction which gives the user direct control. Alongside these developments has been the addition of colour to displays generally and to high resolution displays in particular; colour is seen to be particularly important because of the added real world fidelity given to the displayed images which may be selected by touch. Another development complementing touch is that of videodisc and optical disc technology which can be used, amongst other things, to present animated objects for display and touch control. The interaction method used is a variation of graphics interaction making use of colour and videodisc or optical disc.

Input Requirements - Touching

Touching is indicated to the system by some form of touch screen device. Two categories of these can be distinguished: those that consist of a screen of clear material overlaying the display, and those that consist of sensors surrounding the face of the display. They all operate by transmitting x-y coordinates to the VDU whenever a touch is detected. The touch may be via a stylus but is more usually the user's finger. Some systems can be programmed to monitor continuously the display allowing the user to use the screen for continuous data input as well as for discrete selections.

Screen overlays. There are a number of devices in this group, including the Touch Wire System, Acoustic Ranging, and Conductive Membranes. Since the touch screen device overlays the VDU screen there can be a problem in reduced light from the VDU; in addition the material in the overlay is susceptible to scratching and grease which can limit the effectiveness of the device.

Screen surrounds. There is one device in this class, the Light Emitting Diode (LED) which uses LEDs mounted on the side and bottom of the VDU frame. Parallax problems can occur with this approach, caused by the gap between the VDU display and the LED beams causing the user to miss the correct touch point. This can be corrected by software adjustments.

The touch screen device is integrated with the display, so hand/eye coordination problems are minimal. The user does not have to shift focus from the screen to the input device and vice-versa; hence it minimises interference with the user's normal decision making process. Input is faster than with other devices since hand movement is at a minimum.

Careful design of the display elements is necessary to ensure that the user can read and distinguish the items with comfort when near enough to the screen. Off-screen touch devices are advantageous in this respect since the users may position themselves to optimise independently both viewing the screen and using the touch control device; such a device would mimic the screen contents. This approach would prove advantageous for minimising any possible physical fatigue as a result of reaching to touch the screen. However, this approach would require the user to shift attention between the screen and the control device. It may be that the development of flat screens incorporating a touch screen device would resolve all of these problems.

The use of a touch screen device enables the interaction to present procedures in a controlled sequence; it requires minimal training since the user is guided by the system and touch is the only response necessary. User acceptance of touch screen devices can be high, although users may need to learn that the touchscreen does not always respond as might be expected. In particular, it may not mimick the properties of an electromechanical switch - immediate operation (at less than 100 milliseconds response time) and some form of feedback, either tactile (the switch moves through some form of displacement similar to key travel), audio (the switch emits a click or beep), or visual (the switch changes in some way either in colour, intensity, uses inverse video, blinks, or is underlined). In the absence of these indicators the user can be left with the impression of misoperation and may repeatedly retouch the screen.

Output Requirements - Seeing

An enhanced bit mapped display is the basic element around which the display terminals in this group are constructed; the enhancement is provided by additional bits used in the display process to generate colour. The use of the videodisc or optical disc as a complementary device is also considered since this enables the storage and retrieval of high quality images at an economical rate.

There are three technologies using a disc to store TV images, and these are Capacitance Electronic Disc (CED), Video High Density (VHD) and the Optical Laser System (OLS). The optical laser system is the technology used because the use of a light beam to read information from the surface of a disc means that a single track can be read continuously to generate an apparent still picture. Random access to these tracks is enabled by specifying track number. This enables the user interface to provide the user with control over the progress of the interaction and take decisions at branching points.

The ability to see colour in a display is dependent on the characteristics of the human perceptual system and the technology of the device. In black and white photographs the eye can only distinguish thirteen levels of grey from black to white but it is capable of distinguishing a very large number of colours. True colour blindness is a very rare phenomenon affecting less than one person in a million; much more common is colour deficiency where the eyes cannot perceive particular colours, but even that is not very common. Approximately 8% of the male population suffer from some form of deficiency, and less than 1% of females do.

The graphics interaction method is primarily orientated towards the needs of inexperienced users. The addition of a touch screen and colour enables icons to be used in an enhanced way.

Icons. Control functions can be expressed visually using icons to represent familiar objects. This flexibility of the software and hardware enables these control functions to be displayed with specified colour, shape, location and legend. Icons can be used to represent a wide range of artefacts such as calculators and telephones, knobs and their associated dials. The supporting software can cause the icon to assume the properties of its real-world counterpart; a knob can be "turned" (that is, touched) on, with a dial registering the operating conditions of the component it represents; the calculator can be used to perform calculations by "pressing" (that is, touching) the appropriate buttons; the "telephone" can be used for communication by touching the key pad; and so on. The use of icons supported by a touch screen device provides a degree of real world fidelity at the interface. The legend describing the image can be anything, being determined by the design of the display; it could be upper and lower case text, graphic symbols, foreign language, and so on. In addition, since they are software generated they can be readily modified without impacting the hardware.

Colour. Colour extends the amount of information that can be extracted from a graphics image. It is useful for applications where the user must distinguish rapidly among several categories of data and especially where items are dispersed on the screen or where meaning must be extracted from complex relationships.

Videodisc and optical disc images. The use of the videodisc and optical disc as part of an interaction method can be used to present information in novel ways, exploiting their nature as interactive high quality image devices. Two classes can be identified and these have been described as "new type books" and "new type movies" (Negraponte, 1979). Videodiscs or optical discs used for new type books store images of information equivalent to data stored in a relational and descriptive database; examples include a parts catalogue where the disc can make available specifications and associated subassemblies of a physical part. Similarly, a classified directory could be presented as a film sequence of advertisements. Books proper could be stored on a disc and opened at any given "page" by selecting an appropriate frame. Videodiscs used for new movie types store images of information equivalent to a sequence of film; the difference between the videodisc and film is that the videodisc gives control over the sequence of images to the user; for example, a videodisc could be used to provide training in a given subject where the user could be asked to interact with subsequent sequences depending on the user input. Similarly, they could be used in a route-finding exercise where the user navigates through a filmed sequence.

A spatial data management system (SDMS) was developed at MIT several years ago as part of a programme of research on user-system interaction in novel electronic environments (Bolt, 1979). One aspect of the work was to explore the value of "spatial cueing as an aid to performance and memory" as demonstrated in the "Simonides Effect" (Bolt, 1979). Simonides was renowned in ancient Greece for being able to recite long poems from memory; the technique he used to achieve this was to associate in his mind pieces of the poem with familiar objects in a local temple. Retrieval was achieved by taking an imagined walk through the temple stopping at each familiar object which triggered the memory of the piece of poem. Another aspect of the work concerned the use of a "virtual space" in which the user could arrange objects spatially and retrieve them using spatial cues.

SDMS was established in the MIT Architecture Machine Group's experimental area known as the Media Room. It uses a large screen occupying a complete wall to present a "Dataland" to the user; this consists of a variety of full colour images and sources of data arranged spatially to suit the user. The user can explore Dataland by using the joystick on the right hand arm of the user's chair; movement in any direction causes a "helicopter-like flight" over the surface of Dataland in the direction of the joystick control. Whilst the large screen reflects movement in Dataland, the right hand monitor presents a "world view" of Dataland by always showing its complete status as a single plan view. A "you are here" marker indicates the relationship of the objects on display on the large screen to the world view.

As an alternative tc using the joystick the user can touch any of the objects on the world view display (that is, on the right hand monitor). This causes the large screen to change to display the object selected in full detail. The joystick located on the left arm of the chair enables the user to zoom in and out of the large screen display. This causes the item to increase or decrease in size and detail correspondingly, including colour, sound, and movement.

Objects in Dataland may be of the type that allow user interaction with the data; such data types contain a so-called "key map" which is presented to the user when such objects become fully visible on zooming in. The key map may be a table of contents in the case of a book or document, it may be a time counter dial associated with a television set enabling a user to move to a different time portion of a program. Other data types include "processes" represented as icons of familiar objects such as a calculator or telephone.

The left hand monitor, incorporating a touch screen, reflects the key map and process allowing the user to manipulate them appropriately. For example, the buttons of the calculator can be touched for computation and those of the telephone for communication. Similarly, the contents list of the book can be touched to reveal a particular chapter or page. A data tablet, upholstered to serve as a lap pad, is used to make notes and annotate objects on display; these are then associated with the appropriate object and retrieved every time the object is referenced. The notes can also be made as a spoken commentary through a microphone attached to the data tablet; these are again stored and played back appropriately.

Sound is used in Dataland to provide an added cue to object recognition; as the user approaches an object by traversing the information space of Dataland any sound emitted by the object increases in volume. Hence a user can be guided by sound as well as by space.

Evaluation of the use of SDMS has been limited. It has been reported to show a quick learning time, particularly with respect to navigation using the joysticks; the importance of the auxiliary monitor providing the world view to complement the large screen is stressed (Bolt, 1979). Equally effective is the use of icons within the spatial framework; Bolt reports that users respond by referring to items by their spatial location - for example, "the letter to the right and north of the green square". The third important component is the use of sound to provide an added medium of communication.

Many of the ideas developed in the SDMS Dataland are beginning to be found in commercial systems such as the Xerox Star, Apple Lisa, and Macintosh.

An application of the videodisc was developed (Mohl, 1980) in the class "new movie types" where its purpose was to enable users to learn about unfamiliar locales by "travelling" around at will through sequences of photographic footage. The videodisc contains two representations of a virtual environment, travel land and map land. Users are allowed to explore both interactively. In travel land the users "drive" around, familiarising themselves with the space by seeing real footage previously filmed on location. Mohl calls this surrogate travel.

The user interface is provided by a touch screen along the bottom of the VDU. Icons depict the various functions giving the user control over speed, direction, route, viewpoint and even season of the year. When users want to access additional information concerning a particular location, they simply touch that area of interest; they are then shown a frontal view of the area with any name superimposed and synthesised sound giving verbal information. At that point users have the option of returning to travel or "entering" the area to see an auxiliary slide sequence of cultural and facsimile data.

The map land is maintained simultaneously on a separate VDU, mounted horizontally, and also equipped with touch panel. Here the users can "helicopter" over aerial views of variable scale and resolution using customised navigational aids.

One of the aids is a "you are here" pointer which is automatically updated as users drive around. A route plotter traces the most recent course of travel, with intensity fading away over time. Personalised markers are overlaid on the overview either by the system automatically placing markers at the locations users have accessed or by the users specifying those landmarks found to be their most effective orientation points. The touch screen enables users to set beginning and ending points for a journey such that the system can "chauffeur" them along the best route in the travel land display. The touch screen can also be used to zoom in on any part of the aerial map. User control can be exercised through a keyboard, joystick, and speech recogniser as well as through the touch screen and with equivalent functionality.

The conceptual basis for the interactive movie map has been to provide the user with much of the experience of real world travel and personalised navigational references. Their evaluation in a pilot study showed that users find it easy and natural to drive around in an unfamiliar environment making real-time choosing decisions. The process allows them to construct their own internal representations of the space of the system.

In evaluating the integrated system it is expected that one of the concepts which will prove to be important in the learning experience is the quality of representation, i.e. the travel land accompanied by the map land which allows users to see the same thing from different points of view. Mohl sees the movie map as an analogue for systems where branching through a network of paths is dictated by the topology of the space. Hence the principles can be applied to such disciplines as chemical structures, biological systems and socio-economic patterns. Mohl concludes that the videodisc becomes not just a vehicle for prescribing learning paths, but a reference instrument driven by the user's research interest.

SPEAKING-HEARING

Speaking is the most natural form of human communication using the medium of natural language. However, that which we take for granted since everybody can do it is inherently very complex, requiring an enormous amount of world knowledge and an understanding of human behaviour to be effective. We underestimate this complexity such that we have a high expectation of the performance of speech recognition devices for input to a computer, speech generation devices for output from the computer, and natural language interpreters as the interaction method. This is not to suggest that we should not use such devices until they reach human performance levels but rather that a human factors evaluation be performed of the utility level of these devices to match them to appropriate tasks.

It is certainly not the case that speech communication is the best method to use whatever the task. As Damper, Lambourne and Guy (1984), and Visick, Johnson and Long (1984), have shown, it can sometimes produce impaired performance compared with communication based on keying-seeing. As Labrador and Pai (1984) have suggested, speech may most usefully be regarded not as a replacement for visually-based methods of user-system interaction but as one element in a multimedia environment (discussed further below).

<u>Input Requirements - Speaking</u>

Two main technologies are used to provide speech recognition using either Acoustic Representation or a Knowledge-Source Driven Representation.

<u>Acoustic Representation</u>. This approach applies general signal analysis techniques to the speech signal in an attempt to isolate a unique pattern; this is compared with a stored reference set of patterns representing the words in the vocabulary for recognition. In this way the speech utterances can be identified when a match is found. This approach does not attempt to check the syntax or semantics of the spoken utterances or relate them to the context of the task.

<u>Knowledge-Source Driven Representation</u>. This approach takes into account the dynamic use of language, the environment of the task, and the context of the utterance in order to interpret the spoken utterance. Hence many sources of knowledge about the spoken utterance are taken into account, each level contributing to recognition and making up for deficiencies in information from the other levels.

The development target for all of these technologies is aimed at supporting continuous spoken utterances from any speaker using an unlimited vocabulary. However, a number of stages can be identified in the progress towards this target aimed at providing usable, although limited, speech recognition. These stages are Isolated Word Recognition (IWR), Continuous Speech Recognition (CSR), and for each of these either Speaker Dependent or Speaker Independent forms.

<u>Isolated Word Recognition (IWR)</u>. IWR systems require an identifiable pause to be inserted between each word spoken by the user. IWR vocabulary sizes tend to be small (less than 100

words) but their usefulness can be significantly increased through the use of a state transition network (STN); this subdivides the speech recognition task into a series of connected nodes where the path to successive nodes is determined by the word selected at a previous node. This approach decreases the universe of possible words for recognition, reduces the response time, increases the accuracy level and presents an interface more closely resembling normal speech. This technique is also applicable to CSR systems.

Continuous Speech Recognition (CSR). CSR systems enable the recognition of natural sentences (that is, connected words) without the need for pause insertion.

Speaker Dependent. These systems require that the users train the device to their speech characteristics by reciting each word in the recognition vocabulary. The resulting speech patterns are stored as a set of "templates" for each user. The number of speakers supported by the device is related to the storage capacity of the device.

Speaker independent. These systems are able to accept input from any speaker using the recognition vocabulary; they do not require a training period.

A number of human factors studies have been performed which demonstrate that speech communication is by far the most effective means of human communication, with typewriting (keying) being the least effective. It has also been demonstrated that a "listening typewriter" (Gould, 1980) could be an effective dictation device. However, the level of capability in the technology does not yet permit such applications, rather the particular capabilities of the technology need to be analysed and applied to tasks which can take advantage as appropriate.

The status of development of the technology suggests use of speech recognition when the following criteria apply:

- When the user's hands and eyes are dedicated to the task leading to so-called "head-up, hands-free" applications.

- When the user has high information overload and speech can be used to provide an alternative channel of communication.

- When intermediate steps in the task can be eliminated, such as avoiding the need to stop and key-in data, thus reducing task time.

- When the users are required to move around the task environment.

- When the users are reluctant to use conventional input methods (such as senior managers' reluctance to use keyboards).

- When handicapped users are involved who are unable to use another input medium.

These criteria are useful in directing the use of the technology for a particular task; a number of design guidelines have been developed as a result of human factors studies to direct the design of the recognition vocabulary. They include measures for vocabulary size and choice, feedback techniques, error rate factors, environmental considerations, and training needs where appropriate. Much more work needs to be done however, before the use of these devices can become widespread.

Output Requirements - Hearing

Three technologies are used to generate speech from a computer system and these are Digital Compression, Phoneme Synthesis, and Pre-recorded Speech.

Digital Compression. With this technology a set of spoken words is digitally encoded, compressed and stored. This technique models the human vocal tract by simulating the parameters used in producing speech. However, the result is of moderate intelligibility lacking in intonation quality.

Phoneme Synthesis. With this technology speech is synthesised by concatenating phonemes, the basic unit of speech sound. This technique is the most flexible and does not limit the number of words that can be produced; however, the speech sounds unnatural and is of low intelligibility since it lacks prosodic information.

Pre-recorded Speech. With this technology spoken sentences or phrases can be recorded in full and stored for later "generation". This technique is limited in flexibility, since it requires all words to be generated in advance as sentences, but is of high intelligibility.

One of the primary human factors considerations is the intelligibility of the speech output to the user by the device; in addition, the acceptability of the generated speech may be low because of the mechanical nature of synthetic speech. This is related to the user's perception of the generating device; if the user thinks speech was generated by a machine it reduces the expectation of good performance of the system and increases the tolerance level. Consequently, the choice of voice quality for the generating device is an important consideration.

User performance may be improved by providing options such as the use of a male or female voice, accent, and the speed of response; user frustration is apparent where the system response is at a fixed rate and tone especially for a boring task.

The user's perceptions of the system often seem to be affected by characteristics of the synthesised speech, usually in the following ways:

- Speed of response is related to competence; the faster the response, the more competent the system.

- Speed of response is related to benevolence. A "normal" response (i.e. human level) confers the highest degree of benevolence and any variation in speed is seen to reduce it.

- Acoustic quality is related to learning time. This varies with the degree of distortion in quality.

- Intonation level is related to emotion. Variation provided emphasises the content of the spoken output.

A balance must be held between the method of input and the method of output used by the system so that the user's expectation is not distorted by one mode in terms of another.

Thomas and Rosson (1984) provide a useful review of the literature and suggest a number of design guidelines relating to the use of speech synthesis.

The dominant method of interaction in the speaking-hearing group is the use of natural language. Natural language is a user's normal mode of communication; a system supporting natural language has the attraction of this normal use of a mode which is adaptable and effective.

The development of natural language interaction is essential for the effective use of speech recognition devices and in turn for the development of systems for use by inexperienced users. The successful development of a natural language understanding and generating system requires developments in syntax analysis, semantic analysis, context analysis, and pragmatic analysis, and many problems exist which have to be resolved in each of these areas. For example, consider a problem from semantic analysis: the phrase "a plastic surgeon" could refer to a surgeon made out of plastic or to a surgeon who manipulates skin structures. Consider a problem from context analysis involving ellipsis, that is, where part of a speech utterance is omitted but which can be inferred from the content by the listener; in "John bought a red jumper and Bill a green one" it is clear that the elliptical reference is to a "jumper", however consider a more difficult one in "How many cars were sold in March?" followed by the eliptical query "April?". Here the reference is to "cars sold".

In order to resolve problems such as these, the system must have a great deal of knowledge about the world and user behaviour. It also requires techniques for reasoning about the knowledge. Reasoning has three roles to play:

- In understanding input, reasoning can be used to determine why a speaker made a particular utterance and hence resolve problems in interpretation.

- In reacting to input, reasoning can be used to determine the response.

- In generating the response, reasoning can be used to prepare the response.

Reasoning underlines the central point that natural language is part of a system of intelligent behaviour carried out by humans;

when combined with speech recognition devices, natural language enables speech understanding, and can support effective speech generated response.

An application of an isolated word recognition system has been developed for the Advanced Fighter Technology Integration (AFTI) version of the F-16 plane developed by General Dynamics (Mountford, 1980). The use of speech recognition has particular value in reducing the information overload imposed on the pilot. It provides additional benefit in permitting head-up, hands free operation in limited light conditions which might otherwise have made it difficult to see a keyboard. Although it is a noisy environment the pilot conventionally wears a helmet which incorporates a microphone which can be connected to the speech recognition device. Single word commands can be issued for use in instrument control, navigation and communication; up to 32 word vocabulary is considered suitable. The use of speech recognition for flight control or weapons operation has been ruled out.

A commercially developed natural language known as Intellect has been developed for database retrieval; It was developed by the Artificial Intelligence Corporation, USA (Harris, 1982). Accessing a database using natural language presents a number of difficult problems; principally, there is the enormous gulf in the way the user might see the information as opposed to the way the system actually organises the information. Inexperienced users find it difficult to reinterpret their queries in terms that the system will understand; even if a computer specialist is used as an intermediary there is still the problem of ensuring that the specialist interprets the user's request correctly and (from the system's point of view) unambiguously. A natural language interface is at least able to react immediately to the user's query so that any misunderstanding can be resolved; the natural language can code and decode the user's query in terms acceptable to the database organisation without imposing that burden on the user.

In supporting this capability the natural language interface has to solve a number of problems arising from the user's expectations about the way data are stored. These can be considered in terms of a simple example, such as the request "What is the percent of total sales in each state?" The user expresses the request using terms with which (s)he is familiar and which form part of normal discourse; for example, the use of the term "sales" and "state" does not require the user to do any special coding. The user thinks of the data in summarised form as in "total sales", not in terms of the detailed way in which the database stores them. The user may think in terms of information which is not explicitly stored in the database but which require the system to calculate, such as in the case of "percent of total sales"; the natural language interface needs to recognise such implied calculations. Similarly, the user may expect data to be aggregated over a time series when a request is made for data at a given time interval; again the natural language interface needs to recognise these occasions and take action.

Such systems as Intellect, although giving the appearance of general purpose interfaces, require a considerable amount of tailoring towards a specific database. A lot of development needs to take place before they can be used with any system without such modification.

LOOKING-SEEING

Looking is used by us to locate items of interest and take in information about our environment, whether that information be moving images, other people, or text. Looking is therefore normally considered an input medium to the user. It can also be considered as an input to the system in so far as information about where the user's eyes are looking can be used as a control action by the system.

Looking provides an alternative modality in system communication to support other modes.

Input Requirements - Looking

A technology has been developed known as the "pupil-centre corneal-reflection method" which is able to detect the user's direction of gaze when looking. It uses an infra-red light source to detect the movement of the eye between the pupil centre and the cornea; the signals are picked up by a TV camera and computer-analysed.

Three types of looking can be distinguished from the human factors point of view in this context: spontaneous looking, task relevant looking, and changing orientation looking (Bolt, 1982). Spontaneous looking is that which reacts to external stimuli, such as when objects move. Task relevant looking is that which is governed by the requirements of the task and the visual environment. Changing orientation looking is that which reflects the user's transition between stages of thought.

Where people look provides an index of what they are interested in and where they are going visually to gain necessary information. It can be used in conjunction with a display of objects by the user to indicate selection. Feedback is provided to the user either by a cursor which follows the user's gaze or by a change in the display field. Looking may also be used to complement speech recognition to supplement the information about the item viewed.

An experiment in using eye tracking as an input medium has been performed as a simulation (Bolt, 1982); the view taken in the simulation is of eye tracking as a system component, "eyes as output". A large format display was constructed occupying one wall of MIT Media Room referred to above and consists of a multiplicity of (approximately 20) separate images or "windows". Some of the windows come and go, reflecting their nature as real-time, real-world events. Others are non real-time, some dynamic, and some static but capable of becoming active.

The display represents a senior executive's information world filled with events. Eyetracking is used by the user to control the visual dynamics of the display. The demonstration uses the "pupil centre, corneal reflection distance" technology. The arrangement of the windows is non-regular; the size of the window relects the density of information, and perhaps the importance of its subject matter. The result of the collection of images is a real-time stream of parallel audio visual events laid out in cross section for the observer. The observer selects from this multiplicity by looking. The real-time windows are dynamic; the images are of people talking, gesturing, walking about, of planes diving, cars careering, etc; these dynamic windows react to looking by stopping and then resuming action. The feedback to the user is that they stop to indicate that they know you are looking at them. The non real-time windows such as movies start up when the user looks at them. The user may look away and then come back; the movie resumes where the user left off looking; unlike the real-time windows, the timestream of events waits for the user.

An important aspect of the reactivity of the windows is based on sound. One option is that only the looked-at windows can emit sound or that the soundtrack of the looked-at windows is markedly louder than the other windows. Another option is to play the track of that window currently nearest the observer's view point of gaze plus those of its immediate neighbours in stereo with appropriate fall-off for distance. This tactic would make the observer's auditory focus the looked-at spot in the x,y plane. An alternative way of "neighbouring" at least two sounds is to show proximity not on a "spatial" basis but on a temporal basis, so that those images looked at most recently are juxtaposed auditorally.

Where and how the user looks causes the system to zoom in on some window of interest; at first pass the system cuts to a full-screen view; a further option is to have a "special effects" type of zoom where the frame of the small dynamic window expands to full screen size. Two competing principles determine the stimulus for zooming in. One is based upon zooming automatically after the user has looked at an image for a defined time; the other requires a deliberate action using some other input means such as a joystick, pointing, or speech.

There are two ways in which the user "leaves" a window which is currently zoomed in; one, temporarily for some reason irrelevant to the display, for example someone has entered the room, or the user takes a telephone call; two, when the user leaves the window for the display at large or for some other window. The system takes action related to where the user's eyes go; that is, if the user is distracted the system maintains its current hold; if another view is sought, the system changes. The user is kept aware of the rest of the action when zoomed in by a video "double exposure mix", controllable by the user; that is, a background full view is maintained controllable by joystick.

More recently, Storey and Craine (1984) describe an approach to building a system for the display of animated three-dimensional (stereoscopic) images, in which the perspective changes according to the current viewing position as the user moves his or her head. A demonstration system based on the approach is being built on a grant from the Science and Engineering Research Council in the U.K.

GESTURING

Gesturing, either pointing or gesticulating, with the hands is another form of human communication; it is generally used with speaking to indicate the desired item from a group, such as in "I'll have that one". As such it minimises the amount of voice communication required and increases the efficiency of communication.

Input Requirements - Gesturing

A device for detecting users' gestures has been developed as a prototype (Bolt, 1980). It is based on measurements made of displacements in a magnetic field. One device remains static in the gesturing environment, another is strapped to the user's wrist; the displacement between these two devices in the magnetic field generated is used to determine where the user is pointing. Feedback is provided to the user by a cursor which complements where the user is pointing.

Gesturing is another form of selecting and touching although the technologies are not as well developed as for these other forms of communication; its experimental use to date has been to supplement speech recognition, where the deficiencies in the technology can be compensated by the additional information provided by gesturing. For example, if a user points to something and says "that", the speech recognition device only has to recognise a single word. In the absence of gesturing the recognition device would have to interpret a lengthy description (Bolt, 1980).

A system has been developed at MIT to evaluate the joint use of gesturing and speech recognition as input media at the user interface (Bolt 1980). The aim was to determine how each modality could augment input from the other. The demonstration became known as "Put that there" since it involved the significant use of pronouns in the recognition vocabulary coupled with gesture to indicate the objects referenced. For example, the system would display a screen of objects to the user who might then say "put that" (pointing to an object) "there" (pointing to a desired location); the system would respond by physically moving the object referred to, to the position indicated by the user's gesture. It can be seen that communication in this manner is extremely efficient and takes full advantage of the user's natural ability to indicate position by pointing while minimising use of the limited capacity of the speech recognition device.

"Put that there" was established in the MIT Architecture Machine Group's experimental Media Room. The speech recognition device used is based on Connected Speech Recognition technology which is able to recognise up to five words in each speech utterance; the vocabulary size is 120 words. The gesture-capture device used is based on measurements of a nutating magnetic field; the user has one component of the device strapped to the wrist and the other components of the device remain in a static position. Feedback to the user is provided by an "X" shaped cursor in the position corresponding to where the user is pointing. Output from the system consists of a large screen, full colour, high resolution display; this is complemented by a speech generation device used to query any speech utterances which fail to be recognised by the system. For example, if the user says "Move that there" and the system fails to recognise "Move", the system will respond with the phrase "What command?". This approach directs the user to repeat the required information; this can be compared with a response which simply says "error", which would not prompt the user to provide the information in the correct format and could give rise to user frustration.

The speech recognition vocabulary was structured to complement input by gesturing; hence it comprises pronouns as well as the objects' names. Where the system can interpret speech input without using gesture it will do so, as for example where only one item on display corresponds to the named object, otherwise it will take into account gesture.

A more recent demonstration of how gesturing can be used effectively comes from the work of Lamb and Buckley (1984) who report on a music composition system for children in which the children indicate what they want the computer to do by gesturing in ways that seem obvious to them, using a finger on a graphics tablet, a mouse, and other devices. (The system is modified in an evolutionary way to incorporate gestures that the children feel are the "obvious" ones to use.)

These demonstrations illustrate the value of providing gesture not only as an aid to interpreting user input but in giving the user an interface which parallels his or her normal and "obvious" means of communicating.

MULTIMEDIA INTERACTION

User input and output would benefit from devices supporting the whole range of human communication involving keying, selecting, touching, speaking, looking and gesturing for input, and seeing and hearing for output. The essence is to enable the user to use any of the devices without constraint according to the user's preferences and skill, appropriate to the demands of the task. Of course, some devices are more suited to some tasks than others but this should not limit the objective of providing context-free device use. It follows that where different devices are used to achieve the same action, the effects should be consistent across the range of devices; this so-called "modeless" interaction is an essential pre-requisite for multimedia uses.

Similar comments apply to the interaction methods to be used to exploit the input and output devices; whilst a clear target is to provide an effective natural language interface, similar challenges exist in developing graphics interaction methods. Perhaps the biggest challenge lies in the development of adaptive interfaces which are able to adapt intelligently to the user's skill level and in some senses learn about the user's performance. The success of adaptive interfaces will rest in their ability to develop and maintain a model of the user and of the task domain. The user's model enables the system's knowledge of user performance to grow; the task model enables the system to react to any difficulty the user may have with the task in order to take appropriate action.

To achieve these developments requires a thorough human factors evaluation of the capabilities and limitations of the devices and a greater understanding of the cognitive characteristics of the users. Only then will multimedia interaction with adaptable interfaces be an achievable goal.

AREAS WHERE RESEARCH IS NEEDED

Advances in technology mean that a variety of different "species of interaction" between the human and the machine will be possible in the electronic office environments of the next five to ten years. Research is needed in three related areas:

- to ensure human-machine cognitive compatibility in the interaction between the user and the electronic system

- to develop psychologically optimal building blocks for building user-system dialogues

- to develop a dialogue design methodology suitable for researching and implementing new Human Factors concepts in user-system interaction.

Human-Machine Cognitive Compatibility

The various "species of interaction" that are becoming possible differ in the attentional, memory, and other cognitive demands they make of the user. The various species differ in how appropriate they are in different circumstances, relating to the nature of the task and the nature of the user. And wherever a particular species is appropriate in principle, an indefinitely large number of particular dialogues can be constructed - most of which will be sub-optimal in terms of how well they "mesh in" with the way the human is designed.

The human is designed to be very adaptive to its environment and has shown itself capable of learning to cope fairly well even with what any reasonable person would consider very poorly designed human-machine dialogues. Even so, the onus is on the designer of electronic products to try and optimise their design as far as possible, so that the design fits in well rather than poorly with the way the human is built. In terms of the flow of communication between the user and the electronic office system, this means designing the dialogue to be compatible with the cognitive make-up of the human.

In designing for cognitive compatibility, it is not necessary to start from "square one". Indeed, it would be wasteful and inappropriate to do so since a great deal of research, amounting to thousands of person-years, has already been done on the cognitive psychology of the human being. This research has been done in the academic institutions over the last twenty-five years or so and should not now be overlooked.

Much of mainstream cognitive psychology may be of only indirect applicability to the problem of user-system interaction. There is a need to review what has been done in cognitive psychology, identify what can be applied, and research methods for "packaging" what is known in a form that can be used by designers of office systems without them having to become cognitive psychologists themselves.

Optimal Building Blocks

One very practical way, amongst others, of packaging what is known about optimal dialogue designs (whether or not the knowledge is based on research in cognitive psychology as such) is to make dialogue building blocks available as code and as specifications for code.

These building blocks would be "micro-dialogues" that could be fitted together to build up more complex sequences of user-system dialogue. They would be, for example, optimal designs for particular kinds of menus, for particular aspects of windowing, for particular instances of speech command - in short, they would be the elements within the various "species of interaction".

The building blocks should not be defined arbitrarily but should be based on a careful psychological analysis of what are the basic "units of behaviour" within an electronic office environment. This aspect of the research links with the work on functional analysis discussed in the previous chapter.

The building blocks should be validated in controlled human

factors experiments and in simulated "real office" situations, including the CAFE OF EVE discussed in the previous chapter. Once available, they would serve two main functions:

- to make optimal designs available to designers for use in building up complex dialogues

- to reduce the need to write new code - to "reinvent the wheel" for each and every new product.

The provision of such building blocks would therefore be an important contribution to standards for user interface design.

Dialogue Design Methodology

The availability of standard, optimal building blocks would facilitate the design of a new product. However, the overall dialogue built up from the building blocks would still need to be constructed and evaluated. Also, the building blocks themselves need to be designed. A dialogue design methodology is needed for both of these purposes.

A key element in such a methodology needs to be a formal Human Factors Language for specifying a dialogue design. This language needs to go beyond existing languages to incorporate human factors concepts at an appropriate level of detail to support communication between the human factors specialists and the team doing the coding. The language should also be sufficiently detailed to allow automated or manual human factors evaluation of the proposed dialogue to be conducted.

Automated methods for evaluating dialogue design specifications produced by the Human Factors Language also need to be researched. This relates to the "packaging" of cognitive psychology referred to above. The aim would be to develop automated methods which the designer could use to apply what is known about human cognitive psychology in order to evaluate proposed dialogue designs, which could then be improved by making suitable modifications. The ability to apply the evaluation methods to written specifications rather than actual software would be economical in terms of time and effort.

A package to allow the designer to rapidly produce an interactive mock-up of the proposed dialogue design (complete with actual screen layouts, and so forth) would also be an important component in the overall methodology. This would mean that once the written specifications have been optimised as far as possible, they could be evaluated in more detail in controlled experiments, using interactive mock-ups. The package should ideally be closely linked to the Human Factors Language and the Automated Evaluation Methods referred to above, which existing dialogue design packages are not. Even so, existing packages are useful in that they allow dialogue designs to be developed and examined relatively easily and in a relatively interactive way, and they could provide useful conceptual inputs. A number of such packages exist and the following are just a few examples: SYNICS2 (Edmonds and Guest, 1984); DMS (Hartson, Johnson and Ehrich, 1984); and SET from PA Management Consultants. SET is a commercially available system which as well as allowing dialogue designs to be mocked up for evaluation purposes is capable of producing actual code for applications packages.

SUGGESTED FURTHER READING

Flocon, B. (1985)
Multimedia user interface at office workstation: speech recognition. In J. Roukens and J.F. Renuart (eds.) ESPRIT '84: status report on ongoing work. Amsterdam: North-Holland for the Commission of the European Communities, pp. 315-325.

Naffah, N., Kempen, G., Rohmer, J., Steels, L., & Tsichritzis, D. (1985)
Intelligent workstation in the office: state of the art and future perspectives. In J. Roukens and J.F. Renuart (eds.) ESPRIT '84: status report on ongoing work. Amsterdam: North-Holland for the Commission of the European Communities, pp. 365-378.

Nebbia, L. & Sandri, S. (1985)
Multimedia user interface at the office workstation speech interface - speech synthesis. In J. Roukens and J.F. Renuart (eds.) ESPRIT '84: status report on ongoing work. Amsterdam: North-Holland for the Commission of the European Communities, pp. 327-335.

THE NEXT CHAPTER

In the next chapter we consider the overall framework, from the user's point of view, within which the basic building blocks of user-system interaction need to fit. This overall framework is the user's model of the system.

CHAPTER 4:

THE USER'S MODEL OF THE SYSTEM

INTRODUCTION - ALTERNATIVE REALITIES

This chapter considers the overall framework within which the basic building blocks of user-system interaction discussed in the previous chapter need to fit. It makes a distinction which is important in practice between the following two concepts.

- The framework which the designer of the system tries to provide for the user. This is called the designer's user model. It is how the designer wants the user to see the system. It is intended to make the system understandable and easy to use. It may be based on a metaphor, such as the use of the desktop metaphor in the Apple Lisa and Macintosh, or it may not be. Often, it incorporates concepts used in competitive products so the product is readily seen to belong to a particular class of such products, with some novel features added to make the new product distinctive. Ideally, it should incorporate the findings from relevant human factors research; often, in the absence of directly relevant research or for other reasons (e.g. pressure of time, precluding appropriate research being undertaken) it relies heavily on the designer's own intuitions based on previous experience.

- The user's working model. This is not the same as the above. It is the internal representation of the system which the user is assumed to have - the user's "mental model" of the system. It will be influenced by the designer's user model, but it will develop as the user learns what the designer's user model is. How rapidly the user learns this will depend on many factors, including how well designed the designer's user model is, and what experience the user has had of other products whose designers have presented similar user models (for example, learning the Macintosh is facilitated by previous experience with the Lisa, since the user models in the two products are similar). With sufficient experience of the product, the user may discover things about it that the designer did not know about or build into the user model. Some of these will be called "bugs", whilst others might just be "interesting features". They form the basis for many of the "tips" and "helpful hints" that are shared through user groups and user magazines. In this way, the user's working model can and often does grow to incorporate elements that are not in the designer's "user model".

What Constitutes An Interface

Consider a hypothetical demonstration system. Its interface is designed to demonstrate the various features of the system by means of examples. It works, but only to a limited degree; for example, it can only handle very small databases, and it has to simulate some functions such as communications between different workstations. A potential buyer or user of the system might be very interested in seeing what could be demonstrated. It would give a better idea of what the final system might look like than a description on paper could do. Apart from exploring the demonstration for this sort of purpose, however, no sensible person would invest much effort into trying to use the system "for real". Such a person, so long as he or she realized it was a demonstration system, would quite rightly expect the system to be limited and to fail in various ways if attempts were made to use it for real work. This would be true even if the interface as demonstrated using the examples looked identical to the final, real system (which we may assume the person concerned would be happy to use). The difference lies not in the appearance of the interface but in the beliefs which the user has about it.

The user must make a lot of assumptions when using a system - assumptions about long term properties as much as about the immediate reactions - in order to be able to use the system appropriately. In order to use a system effectively and to be able to exploit the properties of the system well for his or her intentions, the user is not free to make arbitrary assumptions about it. The assumptions must relate meaningfully to the way the system actually behaves. The "user model" which the designer provides for the user must explain the behaviour of the system and facilitate the user's learning of an appropriate working model of how the system operates.

Parts of the User Model

There are three main areas the user model must cover:

- The long term structural dependencies, i. e. the dependencies between different user sessions in terms of "declarative" aspects - "what is" rather than "what happens" (the procedural aspects). It may be assumed that this information is held in the user's "long term memory". This memory includes information about the "objects" in the system (the sets of information in the system that are discernible by the user), and the relationships between those objects.

- The long term procedural dependencies - "what happens" rather than "what is". As well as knowledge of structural dependencies, the user also needs to carry in long term memory knowledge about what procedures to follow in order to accomplish what effects.

- The session context. During a working session, the user needs much auxiliary information. It is highly dynamic and its structure varies widely between different sessions as well as different systems. It includes information about the status of particular sub-tasks, current priorities, and so forth. This information forms part of the information in the user's "working memory".

Alternative Realities

The basis of every interface design is finding the appropriate concepts for the user. They need to be appropriate in at least three respects: an appropriate number, appropriate meaning, and appropriate level of abstraction. The concepts developed and incorporated into the user-system interface present the user with a view of reality. For the user, it _is_ reality; there is no other system, from the user's point of view, than the system as portrayed by its user-system interface.

It is in terms of this reality that the user must solve the problem of using the system to its best advantage in order to accomplish the work that needs to be done. As for other sorts of problems, this kind of problem solving may be considered to be the achievement of an intended situation - a goal (see chapter 2) - from an initial situation in the presence of an obstacle to be overcome. Usually, for both the initial and the final situation there are many equally valid different ways of describing the situation; these may provoke quite different sorts of associations in the mind of a pondering problem solver, and different levels of success. It has been shown, for example, that people are sometimes more successful at solving problems if they are presented in a concrete way than in an abstract way. The following is a typical example of this effect (based on tasks invented by Wason and Johnson-Laird, 1972).

The subject in the experiment is presented with four cards displaying the following symbols: E K 4 7 . The subject is told that each of the cards has a number on one side and a letter on the other. The subject is then asked to consider the following statement: If a card has a vowel on one side then it has an even number on the other side. The subject's task is to turn over the cards one by one in order to find out whether the statement is true or false, turning over just the minimum number of cards needed to solve this problem.

In an alternative version of this task, the subject is presented with cards which bear the following words: Manchester Sheffield Train Car . The statement to be evaluated is: Every time I go to Manchester I travel by train.

The logic of the two tasks is precisely the same. There is no difference, but subjects in such experiments generally do better in the latter situation where the task is presented in a concrete rather than an abstract way. Both tasks are real tasks, and identical in terms of their logic, but the subject does better with one kind of reality than with the other. Possible reasons for this are discussed by Johnson-Laird (1983, pp. 29 - 34). The important point here is that user performance in the problem-solving situation of using an electronic system can be expected to depend upon how reality is presented to the user.

The development of the concepts that need to be incorporated in the interface design can be considered, as a convenient simplification, to proceed through three steps: they originate from an interpretation of the "real world"; they are made manifest in the user-system interface; and they are learned by the user. Each of these stages introduces its own simplifications, elaborations and distortions. Yet each is a kind of reality. It is debatable to what extent the "real world" can usefully be considered to exist separately from these alternative realities. And it is debatable as to what extent it is useful to consider the alternative realities to differ in their status, their "degree of reality"; they are all equally real to those concerned. What is reality to the system's designer is one thing, what is reality to the user is no more and no less than the user's model of the system. In terms of predictive power, the user's model may sometimes be more useful than the designer's, because complex systems (even as simple as home computers) will behave in ways their designers did not predict and which the users discover.

There are other alternatives as well. The author who uses a word processing pool may well have a model of the word processing system that is significantly different from the model which the word processing operator has. What the author may believe to be a very trivial task to perform using the system, e.g. altering the pagination of a document to take account of some extra text, may (depending on the particular system) be quite time consuming and complicated for the word processing operator. Conversely, the author may waste time performing some operations that could be done much more efficiently by the word processor, e.g. changing "Commission" to "Commission in Brussels" throughout a document.

THE DESIGNER'S "USER MODEL"

When a system is being designed, the designer must decide on a way of presenting the system to the user that is going to be helpful. This is the designer's "user model". It may be based on human factors experiments, and often it is based on the designer's own judgement, which in turn may often be based on practical experience in the past. The design largely depends on the designer's interpretation of the real world and on his or her interpretation of the purpose the system is intended to serve. These two factors primarily influence the decision about which objects the system is going to support, and which structures are going to relate them. Other decisions about the interface also follow from these.

In order to construct an interface that can be explained rationally, the designer must make decisions about which aspects of the system to make visible to the user and which ones to hide. The user should not, for example, normally be aware of the internal encoding of data but it may, for example, be necessary to include in the user model a maximal number limiting the range of numbers that may be expressed at the interface. If for some reason different internal encodings must be used, the designer must make sure the interface is consistent, though the maximal number that can be encoded may be different between the two. As (s)he filters the set of conceivable assumptions, separating those which are part of the interface from those which are not, the designer constructs the "user model".

Different Classes of User

The user model constructed by the designer is, by definition, fixed once the design has been completed (apart from deliberate iterations in the design process). This is not true of the user's actual working model of the system which will evolve as the user becomes more familiar with the system. As mentioned above, the user's actual working model may come to have more predictive power than the designer's in some respects - either the designer's personal working model of the system, or the "user model" that the designer set out to design for the user but which in some respects the user may go beyond.

A designer may decide to develop more than one user model for the system. It may be desirable to conceal some aspects of the system from some of the users though it may be necessary to permit some other users to observe these aspects. The same users who may be able to observe more in one area may be shown less in another. The construction of several user models implies the introduction of different user classes corresponding to those different user models.

An example of a system with distinct user models might be a central corporate computing system with different interfaces for data typists, clerical staff and operators. The data typist usually neither can observe whether other users are on the system, nor how the information (s)he is typing in is spread across the physically distinct storage devices. Clerical staff who may have access to an electronic mail system may have a facility to find out which other participants in the mail system currently maintain a session on the system. They, too, normally have no notion of physical storage devices. The user model provided by the designer for the system operator may, in contrast, include storage devices as an explicit concept. On most systems these are not an isolated add-on concept but are related to the objects which the other users think contain their data in conceptually homogeneous permanent storage. Thus, the system operator can tell the effects of changes in the physical configuration in terms of these objects.

Another example is the interface for the head operator on the IBM system 5520. While for other users the mailing system works transparently, i.e. they only name the document and the addressee, the head operator is aware of the different communication links available. (S)he must decide on the routing of messages, may define different classes of service (such as immediate forwarding, forwarding when the communication link is set up anyway, or forwarding whenever a certain volume of data has accumulated), and may assign privileges to the users concerning which type of service shall apply to their mail. As always when an interface provides extensive opportunities for manual tuning of the system, the user model gives a relatively deep insight into the functioning of the system.

Different user classes and the corresponding different user models are almost always associated with different roles in the organization (see chapter 2 for a discussion of different office workers' roles). The concepts used in different user models must be appropriate for the corresponding group of members in the organization in two respects: concepts concerning the real world must correspond to the view of the real world which may be expected of that user class. People in the sales department, for example, might consider the relation between sales and customers to be the one of foremost interest, while the marketing department might be more interested in the association between sales and products.

Typically, personnel in different user classes have different qualifications and skills. The characteristics of the concepts used in user models must take into account the typical qualifications and skills of users in the corresponding user class.

Finally, the scope of the user model, i.e. the set of concepts included, must be appropriate for the task the corresponding user group must fulfil within the organization. The proportion of the system shown to a class of users determines the scope of their understanding of the system, of their understanding of their role in the context of the entire community of users, and the scope within which they can manipulate the information contained in the system.

This means, amongst other things, that if there are sufficiently qualified personnel, the criticism that computerization would turn them into slaves wholly dependent on the system may to some extent be countered by the provision of a user model of sufficiently large scope. Indeed, limitations on the competence of office staff resulting, for example, from lack of information, or from the need to coordinate with other departments (which in a non-computerized organization is usually done by restricting certain decisions to higher levels in the organization) have been alleviated by the provision of user models providing more scope for selfreliant work than there was in the previous non-computerized organization. This type of job enlargement may increase job satisfaction if the personnel in the user group concerned are sufficiently qualified.

Granularity of User Models

Including a further concept into a user model usually makes it necessary to relate it to many of the concepts already contained in that user model so as to arrive at a new consistent model, often resulting in a considerably more complex new user model. This means in practice that a user model can generally only be extended in fairly large, discrete steps. This is in contrast to the user's actual working model which can grow continuously as the user gradually becomes more and more aware of how his or her different experiences with the system interrelate. Also, for a given user model, individual users may not care to develop their actual working models for aspects they are not interested in. For example, in the case of a multi-service office workstation the designer will have to provide the user with a user model for each of the various services (e.g. word processing, electronic mail, personal filing, corporate database access) and for the system as a whole, but a particular user may choose to learn how to use (to develop an actual working model of) only the word processing service.

Components of the Model in Office Automation

Every system has its own user model which its designer has created for it. Nevertheless, there are typical concepts and characteristics that apply to many or all models. These fall into two broad categories, concerned with (a) the static aspects of the model, and (b) the dynamic aspects.

Static aspects. For all systems which preserve information from one user session to the next one, the user model provided for the user by the designer must explain which objects there are or can be, how they come into existence, what data they contain, and how they are deleted. The explanation of the objects is inseparable from the explanation of the structures which relate objects to one another. Apart from the objects serving the purpose for which the system has been designed directly, such as for example text files or accounting data, there are other objects which help the user to handle the system. Examples would be directories, procedures or profiles. For those objects for which only little structure is implied by the system, the user model needs only to explain the structure up to that level; for objects with high level structure built-in to the system, the corresponding part of the user model must be quite elaborate. An example of the former type would be a text object which might consist of characters making up words which in turn form sentences and paragraphs; an example of the latter would be a database containing sales information, wage data, and accounting information - relating them in a way which allows the evaluation of, for example, profits, taxes, exploitation of capacities and the like. In the latter case this structural part of the user model is often defined independently in a separate document called the "data model" or "information model".

If there are different types of objects, for example text documents and tables, the user model must make it clear how they can be related, or whether the contents of one such object may be transferred into an object of the other type, and what information must be added or is lost in that case. A typical table, for example, consists not just of the numbers contained in its fields, but also of the rules about how some of the numbers depend on others. If a table is converted into text, these rules may be lost. Another example is the way in which in a system like the Lisa allows the user to store a document in a folder, the folder in another folder, that folder in another, and so on, with the final folder being stored away in the "profile". These relations may be defined by the system's behaviour, but they may not become clear to the user unless they are explained explicitly.

During a user session, the system builds up additional information to control the user session. To be able to explain the behaviour of the system during a session, part of this information should be included in the user model provided by the designer. This part is called the session context. (On some systems, there are transitions between the permanent objects and the session context: in the midst of a user session, the context may be saved whereby it becomes an object, and later the session may be taken up again from exactly the point it was saved.) The central part of the session context are the "currencies": the system knows which objects the user is working on currently; it knows the current position within the object; if there are different sets of abbreviations, the system knows which ones are currently in use; when the user is working on a text document, it knows whether the user is currently in insert mode or overstrike mode; and so on. In systems which maintain a hierarchy of directories, there may be a current directory which saves the user, when (s)he speaks about an object, from having to identify it uniquely within the entire realm of objects; it suffices to single it out amongst those reachable from the current directory. Another frequently encountered item in the session context part of the user model is previous arguments: within a user session, the system may remember the last search argument, the last piece of text deleted, the addressee of the last item of electronic mail which was sent out. The user may then make use of them when issuing the same command again or a related command or function.

It should be mentioned that some systems providing updates of a database online are a special case: in order to avoid problems when the system is restarted, they minimize context or in fact provide no session context, mainly for technical reasons. Some systems provide the session context not as an unstructured mass of detail, but their user model introduces intermediate objects giving additional structure to the session context. A typical example would be the window concept used in all the mouse interfaces: each window has associated with it a position on the screen, a position in the object accessed through it, a scaling determining the size at which the contents of the object are being represented, and it also shows the type of the object accessed. In other systems, too, items of the session context exist in multiple instances, but the multiplicity may be haphazard. For example, there may be several working documents, and there may be a position associated with each of them, but there may be only one instance of the cursor mode; if the user in one document enters the insert character mode and then switches to another document, the insert character mode may still persist, though when (s)he last used that document (s)he may have been in overstrike mode.

A special challenge to the designer of the user model is system crashes. Unless the system has been designed very carefully, the user, when restarting the system after it has crashed, may find objects in an inconsistent state. To get them back into a consistent state, (s)he may have to make assumptions which are not part of the user model as intended by the designer, or which have not been integrated into it properly.

Dynamic aspects. The user model not only serves to explain statically the items in the user's electronic environment or on which the system's behaviour depends, but it also must include the dynamic aspects of the system, i.e., given a complete (static) description of the situation at a given moment, and given a specific user request, the user model must imply the resulting situation. In order to be able to use the system purposefully, the user must be able to know what options are available and be able to predict the system's behaviour.

Systems use "modes" restricting the range of functions applicable. The same function or function key may have different effects depending on the mode. If the user intends a manipulation which cannot be accomplished using only one function, (s)he must be able to plan the sequence of steps to follow through to bring the desired effect about. The user model must be sufficient to make such plans.

An example of two modes which occur in many word processing systems are the two cursor modes "insert character" and "overstrike". The effect of the alphanumeric keys depends on them: in the overstrike mode, the letter indicated by the key stroke replaces the letter pointed at by the cursor. In insert character mode the letter is inserted before the letter pointed at and the characters to the right are all shifted by one position to the right. An example of a rather complicated structure of modes would be SOS, while the dependencies in the Lisa and Macintosh systems are more transparent: the choices not applicable in a given mode remain in the menu, but they are shown in grey, while those the user actually may pick are shown in black.

In many systems the user must be aware that there are different copies of the object or of parts of the object (s)he is manipulating. For example, a manipulation may at first only modify a screen buffer, leaving the object proper unchanged, yet at certain points in time, the object itself will be updated. On most systems, it is an illusion to suppose that such subtle points would be transparent to the user and could be omitted from the user model. Not only do crashes make the user painfully aware of the difference between the buffer and the object, but normally many other points would become inexplicable, too. For example, "undo" operations may only work while changes are restricted to the screen buffer - and when space on the permanent storage medium is about to be exhausted major insertions may still be possible in the buffer but the update of the object may fail.

Mouse interfaces use the concept of "blanko" objects imitating for example the writing pad from which the user can "tear off" blank sheets of paper. There are two ways to get hold of such an object: one has the effect that the following manipulation affects the entire "pad", in the other case only the top sheet will be changed.

Another important point in the dynamic part of the user model is the binding of names. Names are strings of letters denoting objects. When the user invokes a long or complicated function or procedure providing a name, it may make a difference whether, while the procedure is at work, the name of the object is passed on or the object itself; this is because by the time the function accesses the object, the association between names and objects may have been changed. Similarly, in procedures the context with respect to which a name will be resolved may be defined at compilation time by including the full path name, or it may depend on a current directory included in the session context. Generally, all functions which manipulate the session context and make use of it at the same time very much depend on the point in time at which this reference to the session context takes place.

The discussion so far has been restricted to a type of interaction between the user and the system in which the system waits for the user's input and the user waits for the system's response. (Should the user input before the system has reacted the system interprets the input as though it had been entered in response to the system reaction.) Each such stream of interaction is called a dialogue. If there are other activities going on of which the user must be aware, more than one dialogue must be conducted concurrently. Examples would be background tasks which may require user input in response to error messages, or a printing task giving a response once the printout has been completed, or indication that there is incoming electronic mail. The user model must distinguish between interleaved dialogues and their respective contexts. The user model must make it possible for the user to know to which dialogue a given input or system response refers.

Helpful Properties of a User Model

The user model provided by the designer should be natural and convincing. A burdensome translation between the user's normal way of understanding objects in the real world and the concepts (s)he can use in the electronic environment will make a system unattractive for the user whilst a better correspondence will help to make the use of the system appear natural.

A similarly natural correspondence between the functions of the session context and the tools or procedures of a conventional office may be used to avoid the introduction of new concepts. It is not yet clear, though, whether these concepts are optimal, or whether it might be better for professional users to familiarize themselves with a new and different tool. This is an area where research is badly needed.

The user model must be easy to learn. This means that it must be easy to acquire any new concepts involved, but also that there should not be a host of facts which must be remembered. The user model should be teachable and it should be self-enforcing, i.e. when the user's actual working model of the system deviates from the model provided by the designer, then (assuming the user's working model is in error and that the designer's user model is helpful in regard to the system behaviour concerned) the behaviour of the system should give the user reason to adjust his or her working model to the user model provided by the designer.

The user model should be conducive to efficient work. This will include taking account of the cognitive and affective aspects of user-system interaction as well as the purely instrumental (see chapter 2).

The user model must suit a wide range of users. At least within the scope of usage expected for the system, the user model must be optimal or near optimal for naive and expert users, for frequent and casual users, for structuralists and for users who like a cook book approach.

The user model must be as simple as possible, consistent with efficiency of operation (e.g. a dialogue based entirely on extremely long sequences of very simple steps may be easy to learn but most users will probably find it rapidly becomes tedious after the initial learning phase).

Design experience has established properties of user models which have proven valuable to achieve good interfaces. The following are some of the key principles. (The "user model" referred to here is the model of the system which the designer offers the user.)

Consistency and completeness. User models must by definition be consistent and complete as they must correctly explain all the observations the user can normally make. The demand for consistency and completeness refers not only to the features explained by the user model but also to the terminology introduced by it.

An example where user models sometimes fail to be consistent are error situations resulting from the exhaustion of certain resources like storage or from hardware failures: on some systems the error messages given in such situations are not meaningful without inside knowledge not contained in the user model. Another point to be cautious about is determinacy: due to the fact that some of the internal mechanisms of the system are excluded from the user model, alternative system behaviour must be left indeterminate in the user model. Models deciding such alternatives spuriously out of their hat, as they sometimes do, are internally inconsistent.

Tidiness. Arranging concepts and terminology in some haphazard manner may suffice to establish a valid user model, but life becomes much easier if concepts and terminology are arranged in a neat way, and if additional higher level concepts or terminology are introduced. For example, in addition to the current line in a text and the current field in a database and the current coordinate in a drawing, it is generally considered helpful to have the concept of "position" which may be any one of these when explaining a COPY command operating on any one of those objects. The proper abstractions help in having the right associations or in classifying a problem in terms of the concepts provided in the user model.

Minimalness. The user model must be complete (see above), but it should not include unnecessary concepts - concepts in addition to those needed to make it complete. If the user model is not minimal, then the user has to learn superfluous concepts and in many cases these complicate his or her task of developing an actual working model of what the system is doing.

There are two variants of non-minimal user models. One is the necessary consequence of incomplete functionality of the system. If, for example, the user must tell the system which segment of the physical storage medium should be used for a certain data set, then the physical structure of the storage medium and perhaps of the storage device must be included in the user model. If the system allocates the data sets automatically, possibly guided by optimization criteria provided by the user, this part of a user model can be simplified considerably.

The other variant is just insufficient abstraction for a given functionality of the system. For example, in explaining a database query system, it may be helpful at the time of sale if the sales person points out to the prospective purchaser of the equipment that the resulting storage accesses are ordered by the physical locations to which they refer, thereby optimizing the time required to process the query. For the user model, however, it may suffice to point out that the response to the enquiry will contain the data specified.

In practice, the user model may be linked very intimately with concepts peculiar to the particular application domain, sometimes to an extent where it would be possible to speak of an extension of the user model. Such links or extensions may be invaluable for a specific community of users, but they should be left to these users or marketing or salespeople rather than the system designer. Often the user model, as it was constructed by the designer and is manifest in the system, lends itself to quite different and sometimes unexpected extensions. Being aware that extensions are only extensions can be important when it comes to improving the use of the system or adapting it to a changing application.

Orthogonality. The term "orthogonal" was coined in analogy to vector geometry: a coordinate system is considered orthogonal when the projection of any one of the base vectors onto any other one is zero. Speaking in terms of user interfaces, this means that manipulation of properties described by one concept should leave those properties unchanged which are explained in terms of other concepts. For example, in editing a videotex page, the concepts of size, font and colour of text, as they are used in everyday understanding, would be orthogonal, i.e. it is possible to change any one of them without affecting the other two. On some videotex systems, though, the functionality does not correspond to these concepts; changing colour may in some circumstances affect the size of a word. If the system is not orthogonal then the user cannot plan his or her intended sequence of actions step by step. Each time a further step is added to his or her plan, the previous ones must be adjusted to take account of the side effects of the new one, but this adjustment in turn will change the effect to be accomplished by the new last step. It is like buying shares in an empty market: the price on which the buying decision depends, depends in turn on my buying.

In terms of orthogonality within the user model, it may be necessary to distinguish explicitly between concepts in the user model and the functionality at the interface. When the set of functions to be provided at the interface is being designed, there may be a conflict between efficiency and orthogonality. If in a majority of cases the user is expected to desire a combined effect changing the properties associated with different concepts, it may be worthwhile to provide a function producing such a combined effect. In such cases the constituent orthogonal functions should be provided as well. In any case, the concepts in the user model must be orthogonal and the function introduced for reasons of efficiency would be explained using several orthogonal concepts. For example, very frequently files are created for the sole purpose of obtaining a printout. It may be desirable to include a function to print and subsequently delete such files. The component functions, printing and deleting, ought to be available at the interface independently and in addition to the combined function.

Factorisation. Some user models may be defined very concisely by reference to a set of principles which apply generally in many different situations. As an example of such a concept describing system behaviour take the "playground": the playground includes all concepts for typing and editing within one line, i.e. inserting and deleting single characters, deleting words, using abbreviations and the like. (The term "playground" refers to the fact that the user can play around without the system interpreting the input further.) There are many situations in which a playground can be used: when filling in a form, every field may be a playground, when formulating a command, the command and each parameter may be a playground; in a line-oriented editor, editing within one line may be done using the playground concept. The user model of the playground applies in all of these situations.

Other examples of generally applicable concepts would be the HELP function if it may be used in any situation whatever, and allows the return to that situation in the same way each time. Similarly, uniform syntax for numbers, signed numbers, decimal fractions, character strings and the like, or general principles explaining the cursor motion within a form, within a text document, or within the formulation of a command would be further examples.

The static part of the user model may be factorised using generally applicable concepts, too. An example would be the window concept associated with mouse interfaces. Once the user has learned the concepts of location on the screen, size of the window, scaling of the object shown and positioning within the object shown (s)he can manage the representation of any object be it text or a drawing or a chart or whatever.

In a factorized model it suffices for the user to learn the "factors" instead of developing a model for every situation anew. This means (s)he needs to learn less and there is less to memorize. The user can transfer experience from one situation to others.

Constructing a factorized user model is the final consequence of the classical design principle of "least surprise", which is the principle of allowing the user to reason by analogy.

Explicitness. Concepts which it is considered are important for the user to learn should be explicit in the user model which the designer provides. Explicit information about the dynamic aspects of the system is perhaps of greatest importance. Of course, dynamic behaviour itself cannot be "displayed" on one screen. What can be displayed explicitly though, are the modes or other criteria on which dynamic behaviour depends.

Information about the status of the system should also be made explicit. Systems supporting objects of arbitrary contents, for example text documents, must provide a clear distinction between the display of the contents of such a document and the display of information about the system - for example by defining a status line, or by distinguishing between what is inside and what is outside the frame denoting a window, or by choosing different representations for windows showing objects and those showing menus. It thus becomes possible to provide the user with information about the state of the system. It is still too often the case that interfaces exist where the user must remember what the state of the system is in order to be able to interpret the information displayed.

The state of the system is usually only shown implicitly. For example, it may be implied by the choices currently available in the menu, by the shape of the cursor, or by the structure on the screen. The HELP function usually gives its information independently of the situation the user was in when (s)he called for help. Any such implicit information can only be exploited properly if the user has a sufficient understanding of the system. In many cases, even the handbooks do not introduce the concepts in the user model explicitly.

The main reason for not showing all relevant parts of the user model explicitly may often be the lack of space on the screen. This refers particularly to information which ought to be shown continuously; just those parts of the session context which are tiresome to keep track of tend to be displayed with the utmost economies of space, for example margins, tab settings, cursor attributes and the like. When there is no room to display all of the session context continuously, it should be possible to inspect on demand those parts not shown continuously.

Generally, the fewer modes a system has and the more the user model is factorized, the more concise may be the information displayed.

Partial models. Not all users are interested in all types of objects or in all functions of the system. It therefore is good practice to design user models in a way that users do not have to learn about the whole system in order to be able to use just a part of it. If formal training is provided, it is possible to concentrate on a partial model at first, and to provide practical experience through routine application before the next course of training designed to introduce the user to further parts of the user model. Many users prefer routine experience and training to be interleaved.

THE USER'S ACTUAL WORKING MODEL

Development of the User's Actual Working Model

In considering how people learn a complex body of information - such as a user of an office system learning how to use it (learning the "user model" provided by the designer, and possibly other elements) - we can distinguish between the facts that have to be learned and the higher-level structure which relates the facts to a frame of reference. In a human-computer dialogue we can therefore refer to the syntactic structure (the facts), and the semantic structure of the dialogue, which refers to the structure of the tasks the dialogue is designed to assist. A skilled user needs both components for efficient use of the system.

There appear to be different individual styles of learning between individuals. The extremes are the "holist" and the "serialist" styles. Holists are said to learn the structural information first and then aim to "fill in" the necessary facts. Serialists, on the other hand, learn the facts first and then integrate them into a structural understanding.

Corresponding to the two styles of learning, we can identify two philosophies which designers seem to use in providing a "user model" which is intended to facilitate the user's learning about the the system. Either the user can be given a description as to how the system works and from there learn the syntactic details, or the user can be led through examples of the syntax to an abstract understanding. The former of these two approaches is more common, not least because users will spontaneously use analogy to reason about an unfamiliar system. Analogy is the means whereby unfamiliar concepts are articulated in terms of familiar ones, and this tendency is a prevailing human strategy of reasoning.

In learning by analogy (which may be explicit or simply implied by the command syntax and the methods of description), there are two types of information to be learned: a) what syntax does the user need to learn in order to apply the analogy? and b) in what ways do the system and the analogy not correspond? The second question reflects the fact that analogies by definition do not apply in all respects: a word processor is different from a typewriter, as well as having similarities.

When the user has assimilated sufficient information to be able to operate the system (s)he can be said to have developed a working model of the system. However, in a psychological sense it may yet be some time before the user's structural knowledge becomes a concept in its own right, rather than an adapted old concept. This emphasises the practice element in learning cognitive skills: it is not merely the attainment of critical facts that is involved but also the "tuning" and restructuring of existing information. This has implications for the learning of highly complex hierarchical systems in which abstract functions are created from new system concepts themselves; in this case learning must take place in stages in which new concepts are first identified, assimilated and then consolidated, before using them to describe yet more complex functions.

Knowledge about the Real World and Permanent Objects

The user's actual working model should normally correspond as closely as possible to the user model provided by the designer, which in turn is derived from an interpretation of the real world, or at least include that as a subset. Generally some understanding of the real world is a prerequisite for learning about a system. The extent to which such outside knowledge is required, varies greatly. For example, a text system may only presuppose knowledge of what constitutes a character or a word or a sentence. On the other hand, an accounting system usually supposes that the user is familiar with the way real world financial transactions are modelled in the books. Since this modelling process is defined by law, these systems tend to take even the terminology for granted.

Knowledge about the Session Context and Dynamic Behaviour

Given that the user is familiar with the way the contents of the permanent objects relate to the real world, it remains to introduce the novice user to the session context and to the dynamic behaviour of the system. Unassisted exploration of a system by novice users tends to lead to the users developing working models which with respect to the users' very limited experience appear to describe the system, but which later turn out to be inaccurate. It then becomes necessary to rearrange the experience and learning so far, which for many people is a very difficult process. (An incorrect "working model" need not make it impossible to use a system, but there will be points in the system's behaviour which will surprise the user; at such points the effect of the user's action will not be what was intended so (s)he will have to correct himself or herself, which will mean disappointment and extra work.)

Teaching Procedure

Teaching before prospective users have become aware of the problems can have a demotivating effect, particularly if users consequently expect not to make errors when they first use the system. They will make errors and become disappointed. A compromise would be to provide just a framework in terms of concepts and terminology through formal teaching, but to let the user do his or her own exploration and to leave it to his or her own efforts to relate experience to the basic framework. The properties of the user model provided by the designer which make it possible to rely on consistently applicable principles and terminology which would be the basis for such teaching, have been discussed in the previous section.

If there are subsets of the user model sufficient to do useful work, this feature can be exploited in order to divide the learning process into several steps, in line with the idea of "partial models" discussed above. If for reasons of efficiency there are functions shortcutting particular operations then, in line with the discussion above on "orthogonality", these functions should only be used after the more elementary functions have been learned.

The training should take individual differences - e.g. different skills, holist and serialist style of learning - into account.

Self-adapting Systems

There is a special situation when a system changes its behaviour over the course of time, as happens in the case of self-adapting or learning systems. Not all of these changes need affect the design of the user model provided by the designer or have any impact on the actual working model the user develops, but those which do will require further learning by the user. The advantages gained by the adaptation of the system to a particular task or user must then be weighed against the effort required of the user to readjust his or her actual working model of the system.

CONCLUSIONS

The user model provided by the designer must be very carefully designed as it forms the basis for the actual working model which the user develops of the system, and that in turn influences the way in which users can and will make use of the system.

It is not yet common practice to support the user in his or her development of a suitable working model, though much could be done. Sometimes there appears to be no consciously designed user model at all. Typically, handbooks introduce the user model only implicitly. Of the information needed to support the user in developing a suitable model normally only some parts are represented at the interface.

Research would be desirable to find out more about the ways in which individual people differ, and to evaluate the resulting differences in behaviour. Research is also needed to find optimal ways to teach new users. A particularly valuable result of such research would be a list of measurable criteria to aid interface designers in assessing the effectiveness of the user models they provide.

AREAS WHERE RESEARCH IS NEEDED

The way in which people form a model of an electronic environment is a special case of how they form a model of any environment.

There is a need to review what has been learned by psychologists about the models people form of their environments, and how they go about forming them - the factors that facilitate and hinder such learning - and apply that knowledge to the design of suitable electronic environments.

It is important to review what is known about how a person's model of an environment changes as (s)he becomes more familiar with it, and how exposure to different aspects of the environment at different stages of learning can accelerate or slow development of a useful model.

It is important to recognise that there is no single, true model of any environment, but only a set of possible models any one of which may be optimal for certain purposes at particular points in time. Research is needed on techniques for presenting the same electronic system in different ways according to the particular user and the task in hand. The role of metaphor and analogy is especially worth exploring, as is research on the schemas and scripts that people take with them from the paper-based office to the electronic office. Research on how schemas and scripts can become modified and extended to include new elements also needs to be researched in the context of office products.

Research is needed on techniques for facilitating the kinds of learning that users need to do in coming to an understanding of what a system does and how to operate it succssfully. Effective techniques for online learning are particularly needed. Techniques for helping the user when it is clear that the user's current working model of the system requires some revision also need to be developed.

SUGGESTED FURTHER READING

The discussion in this chapter has focussed on what the designer can do to facilitate a user's learning of a new system. It has been noted that what a user learns will be strongly influenced by the "user model" that the designer provides, but it is unlikely ever to correspond exactly to the designer's "user model" - at an early stage of learning about the system it will incorporate only some aspects of the designer's user model, and later it may include elements that the designer did not know about and did not include in the user model; at all stages, it will be influenced by the prior experiences and associated expectations that the user brings to the new system.

The discussion above did not dwell on the structure of the user's learning - the form which the representation of the system "in the user's head" takes. Further discussions of mental models which go into this aspect in more depth can be found in the following.

Gentner, D. & Stevens, A.L. (1983)
Mental models. Hillsdale, New Jersey: Lawrence Erlbaum Associates.

Johnson-Laird, P.N. (1983)
Mental models. Cambridge: Cambridge University Press.

THE NEXT CHAPTER

The previous chapters have been concerned with delimiting the problem, reviewing the technology available for supporting the input and output sides of the user-system interface, and considering the overall view of the system which the designer seeks to present to the user, and which provides the user with a an overall model of the system in which user-system interaction can occur. In the next chapter, we consider how the system presents information to the user, and how users can communicate through the system to exchange information. In the traditional office, this has been by paper, face to face contact, and telephone. In the electronic office a much wider range of possibilities exists.

CHAPTER 5:

SPECIES OF INFORMATION

INTRODUCTION - THE NATURE OF INFORMATION

In chapter 3 we looked at the species of interaction that Information Technology makes possible between human and machine - the flow of control between the two partners involved in user-system interaction, and in chapter 4 we considered the overall control framework in terms of the user's overall model of the system. In this chapter, we turn our attention away from the question of controlling the system and we consider the nature of the information that is being exchanged - away, that is, from "species of interaction" to focus here on "species of information".

Information Technology is first and foremost about information, especially the communication of information (from the machine to the human, from the human to the machine, and from human to human via machines). New electronic office systems must optimize the way in which information is presented by the machine to the user and must facilitate the user's presentation of information to others.

In this chapter we consider the following:

- pertinent characteristics of human information processing
- common species of information
- trends in optimising the presentation of information
- areas where research is needed.

Before moving on to these, we need to make a few basic distinctions, as follows.

Basic Categories of Information

Shannon's communication theory definition of information in terms of overall levels of uncertainty, expressed in binary digits (bits), is useful in assessing technological issues of channel capacity and storage requirements, but it is not concerned at all with the purpose of the communication or the meaning of the information. This type of definition is of very limited value in terms of the human factors of user-system interaction, where it is necessary to consider purpose and meaning, and how well these are achieved or expressed.

Other definitions are frequently too broad - for example, information is "that which is exchanged between components of a system to cooordinate their activities so that the complete assembly behaves in an organised way" (Scarrott, 1979).

For the purposes of the present discussion a functional categorisation of information will be used which distinguishes between the following basic categories:

- data
- structural (or relational) information
- communicable (or substantive) information.

Data

Data are conceptualized as discrete elements of information: the elements within the database. These elements may be conceptualized as aggregations or patterns of bits of information in the communication theory sense. Psychologically meaningful elements of data in the office environment may be in many forms, such as:

- figures
- text
- voice
- graphics
- photographs (image)
- moving pictures (animation).

Data in all these forms may be stored in digital form. The method of storage has implications in terms of capacity, average access time and the system cost per bit. Alphanumeric or other characters entered by keyboard require far less storage capacity than photographic images or moving pictures. However, the rapidly falling costs of storage, as well as improvements in display technology and other technologies, are removing constraints that would otherwise be imposed by this. Systems designed to support creation and manipulation of high-quality colour images are already available (e.g. from Artronics). Systems that allow the user to mix and edit text, image, voice and other forms of electronic representations are already beginning to appear (e.g. from Wang and OTL), and further developments are expected over the next few years.

Structural Information

Structural/relational information is meta-information - information about the structure and relations of the discrete elements of data. The more closely the data structure presented to the user at the user interface corresponds to the user's cognitive model of the domain concerned, the easier it will be for the user to work with the system effectively. It is, however, extremely difficult to consider structure generally, in the absence of the specific context. What constitutes an optimal structure in any given case depends critically upon the "schema" which the user brings to the situation, which in turn depends upon a number of factors including the nature of the information and the purpose for which it is being used.

A "schema" in this sense is a cognitive structure applying to the user's knowledge, specifically the user's expectations about the way in which the substantive information of interest is organised. It provides a mental framework onto which the appropriate elements from the material to be understood can be "attached". It provides a basis for categorisation, selection, deletion, abstraction, consolidation and organisation of information. Once a schema has been learned it can be used to understand other situations which have a similar structure (Thorndyke, 1977).

The importance of schemata in influencing remembering was first identified by Bartlett (1932). More recent illustrations of their importance in relation to the presentation and use of information come from, for example, the work of Geiselman and Samet (1980), and Samet and Geiselman (1981), who have shown how schema theory can be applied to improve the effectiveness of presentation of information.

Communicable Information

Communicable information is the substantive content of the information. In interacting with an information system, communicable information is presented to the user at the user-system interface. It may be presented in a form which makes use of several of the data types indicated above, or the system may allow the same substantive information to be presented in alternative ways (e.g., a table, a bar chart, or some other form of representation). It may be generated by the machine itself, or it may be substantive information that another user has processed and compiled for communication to other users. In principle, the same rules apply to both types of communicable information. It should, however, be noted that information communicated to further users will often be more "packaged", perhaps in the form of a complete report containing a mixture of graphics, text, and images.

The following discussion is concerned with pertinent features of how humans process the information presented at the user-system interface, and the variety of "species of information" which emerging technology makes possible.

HUMAN INFORMATION PROCESSING

The human is not like a photographic plate which can be passively impressed with information from the environment. Human perception and processing is an active process, the human forming hypotheses and seeking information to confirm or disconfirm these hypotheses. In effect, the human cues (prompts) himself or herself, has expectations, and makes a number of assumptions in processing information from the environment.

Levels of Processing

The processing that is involved includes both processes that are relatively easily available to the user's conscious awareness and processes that are not so readily available. The user may often not be consciously aware, for example, of the assumptions he or she is making in interpreting a screen of information; indeed, in many situations it is probably the case that only a small subset of all the assumptions involved are ever made explicit, the majority remain implicit. In line with this view, thought can be considered to be a symbol system of highly abstract concepts, which are concretized or "clothed" in some form such as words or images for communication to consciousness (Arnheim, 1969). The words and images used for communication are imperfect (or necessarily incomplete) representations of a symbol system that is not available to consciousness.

Consistent with this view, work on syllogistic reasoning has shown that people are normally incapable of articulating the processes (or rules) which underlie their actual responses (c.f. Wason and Evans, 1975). Artificial Intelligence work on expert systems has shown a similar general finding - experts typically find it difficult to explain fully the processes by which they arrive at the judgements they make. And in the field of psychotherapy, the communication techniques developed by Erickson (e.g. Erickson and Rossi, 1979) and others reflect the view that information can influence the recipient at different levels, not all of which are obvious to the person concerned at a conscious level.

At all levels, it seems that only some aspects of the total array of information presented are processed at any given time. The user does not attend equally to all aspects of the situation.

Attentional Processes

Apart from the fact that human sensory input and output are necessarily limited in terms of parallel processing (e.g. we can only look in one direction or say one thing at a time), central processing capacity is also poor when dealing with more than one channel of information at a time. This is particularly true when the characteristics of several channels are similar. For example, listening to two conversations at the same time is particularly difficult because of the extra processing effort involved in distinguishing the two sources of information.

Some parallel processing is possible, especially in highly skilled situations such as driving a car and holding a conversation. However, the limitations on processing capacity mean that increases in the difficulty of one task, e.g. driving (e.g. because of traffic conditions), usually affects the other. The conversation becomes more difficult to sustain as more processing resources are allocated to the primary function of driving.

Human information processing systems overcome these limitations by behaving as selective processors. Rather than attempting to process all information as a computer would do, attention is focused on particular aspects to the exclusion of others. The information processed depends upon what is perceived by a person to be relevant, on the basis of available context information. This process is therefore more complex than in a simple data-driven model of a computer, which operates in a pre-programmed way on all data impartially. Unlike such a computer, human information processing is not entirely data-driven but is also a function of what the human is thinking about, as well as preconceptions and prejudices. (Artificially intelligent systems are beginning to incorporate approximately similar characteristics to a limited extent, often in order to facilitate more efficient information processing and sometimes to make feasible what would otherwise not be feasible at all because of the sheer amount of processing that would be involved.)

One way of looking at this strategy is to think of the human mind as subconsciously or implicitly making assumptions about its environment based on previous experience, and as processing information accordingly. The assumptions, which may be modified by incoming data, serve to "de-fuzz" the incoming information by providing a frame of reference or context for it.

The emphasis on cognitive assumptions seems to underlie the frequently quoted necessity for consistency in presenting information. However, whilst consistency is necessary to decrease the processing load and increase efficiency, judicious use of obvious inconsistency can sometimes be used effectively to increase the focusing on and processing of relevant information. A simple example of this might be the use of coloured key words (see below).

The user's attention can sometimes be positively misdirected in subtle ways that may impair the processing of relevant information. An illustration of this comes from Flowers _et al_. (1981) who showed that the inclusion of highly familiar sequences in non-cued portions of a display tended to reduce the accuracy of partial report in the cued section of the display. "Attentional capture" by familiar material may therefore detract from the attention paid to unfamiliar material at another location.

Taking the algorithm analogy for selective attention suggested by Dixon (1981) and the suggestion that the global or overall stimulus properties are the easiest to direct attention to (Miller, 1981), it would seem that consistency in the overall structure of the presentation is desirable but some inconsistency (e.g. colour, emboldening, uppercase) is useful in order to focus attention on key items within that structure.

Even assuming that the user's attention is directed properly, the effectiveness of the presentation will depend upon the "species of information" used. The various "species" that emerging technology makes possible are not all equally suitable for all purposes. The system needs to select a "species" which is best suited to the purpose in hand.

COMMON SPECIES OF INFORMATION

Communicable information can be "clothed" in the following general ways, which provide a broad framework for considering the various "species of information" considered below.

- Symbolic language systems (verbal, mathematical, etc.)
- Static images (pictures and graphs)
- Animated images, possibly combined with verbal information (films and video).

Whilst in practice these overlap, the distinctions are drawn in order to facilitate consideration of the strengths and weaknesses of these broad categories.

Symbolic language systems are particularly useful for expressing complex relationships between elements and ideas. A distinction may be drawn between general purpose symbolic systems and particular restricted symbol systems. The distinction is a real one in terms of the generality of concepts that may be expressed. The primary general purpose language system is the verbal language, which is extremely flexible and general in terms of what may be expressed.

The generality of verbal language is, however, gained at the expense of some precision. More precise symbolic systems (e.g.

mathematics) are in contrast limited in their generality but more precise in their terms. A further limitation of verbal language is that its generality is frequently limited by national and cultural boundaries. Some of the more precise languages, however (e.g. mathematics, programming languages, etc.), are recognisable internationally.

Verbal languages are useful for discussing and associating concepts. Restricted languages (e.g. mathematics) will provide precise descriptions. Graphic representation of the concepts may aid in providing an abstract (e.g. a flow chart, a graph) - a view at a glance of what the restricted language expresses more precisely.

Images and graphical information are useful for showing syntheses and abstractions. Images are particularly useful for displaying atmosphere, expressing a feeling, and representing visio-spatial relationships. Graphs are useful for expressing trends in numerical data, particularly trends over time. Flow charts are particularly useful for expressing sequential and directional concepts, synthesizing relations that may be expressed verbally.

Moving pictures, (video and film) are good for presenting sequences and illustrating ideas, their naturally sequential format of images and verbal message are good for presentations. The introduction of the videodisc, which provides for rapid access of images and for branching rather than the standard single sequential format of video tape or film, provides intriguing possibilities (see below).

Within the broad framework provided by these major categories we can consider the more important of the various "species of information" that are emerging, and which complement the "species of interaction" considered in chapter 3. The more common "species" include:

- text
- voice
- tables
- graphics
- images
- animation.

Text

Text is probably the main means of communicating complex ideas in the office environment. It is primarily sequential and appropriate for conveying a complex series of ideas in a structured and formal format. This does not exclude more informal use of text in electronic messaging and computer conferencing, but merely emphasizes the strengths of this form of representation of information. A feature of text, (and human verbal communication generally) is a high level of redundancy. Much evidence exists to show that little of the text may be read (in the sense that the visual symbols are decoded). Consider this sentence where all the short words have been replaced: "When xxx sun xx shining, girls xxx boys come xxx xx play." The fact that it is intelligible shows that the replaced words are probably little used in reading. Given the redundancy of the text, the strategy is one of taking as few key words or grammatical structures as possible to be in a position to determine the gist of the text. Hence, proofreading for spelling errors is difficult and tiresome: we are not accustomed to reading all the text.

Extracting the meaning of what is read involves several stages of perceptual and cognitive processing, requiring perceptual, memory and linguistic skills. The reader has to process the text at a number of different levels, (individual letters, spelling, syntax and the surrounding context). With fluent readers, and with most text, this combination of skills proceeds smoothly and automatically; but the patterning of them can be easily disrupted, if a further visual/verbal task is imposed concurrently.

Representing textual information therefore requires that consideration be given to:

- theories of reading
- the representation of text in memory
- presenting text on the VDU.

Theories of reading. Hochberg (1970) presented one of the most influential theories of reading. The theory suggests a two-process model of reading, distinguishing peripheral search guidance (PSG) and cognitive search guidance (CSG). During fixation the eye has a clear area of vision extending around the fovea; beyond about 10 letters each side of the fixation only broad characteristics of the word are available. PSG detects gross physical features in the periphery, initiating saccadic eye movements to bring relevant features into the foveal region so that high order cognitive processing can occur. CSG in turn provides PSG with more global information about what cues are to be expected.

La Berge and Samuels (1974) argue that fluent reading depends on automatic processing. If the reader has to devote extra attention to a low level process such as deciphering a word, fewer resources are available to process information at a higher level. This argues that efficient presentation of text should avoid the use of any distracting simuli, such as unusual word fonts, unsystematic use of colour, flashing characters, etc. Conversely, this research suggests ways in which the attention of the user may be captured. (One of the problems experienced with ZOG, a menu-driven computer information system, is that users often fail to read what is on the page displayed - Robertson et al., 1981). Care should be exercised in generalizing from the research that has examined reading from the printed page, since computer-generated text may both offer new possibilities and restrict some of the possibilities available with paper, such as:

- A quick perusal of a paper document allows one to gauge both length and structure. (Similar facilities are available on both the MIT dataland system and the Star-type systems, but are not available on some other systems, e.g. Prestel.) The form of such facilities has not been experimentally researched, and there has been no work that considers alternative solutions.

- Computer generated text does, however, facilitate a number of opportunities that were more difficult to provide with non computer-based technologies, including:
  - the use of colour for coding and emphasis
  - different fonts for coding and emphasis.

Representation of text in memory. The importance of considering the representation of text in memory is to examine the case for representing text in such a way that it will facilitate memory for the information. Garnham (1981) suggests that text is represented at neither semantic nor linguistic levels, but rather as a mental model that contains representation of only those individuals and events that are relevant to interpretation of the text in question. These results suggest an "associational" representation and are, perhaps, a function of the story type of text used in the research. The inference that may be drawn, however, is that an associational type of structure, using coding by colour or location may sometimes enhance memory for text. This "enhanced" writing format needs experimental verification.

Representation of text at the interface. Quite a large body of research has considered the representation of text at the interface. This may be broadly broken down into three categories, concerned with: legibility; presenting "pages" or frames of textual information; and continuous reading. The bulk of research has considered videotex systems. Issues of text legibility have received the largest amount of research attention; an excellent summary is provided by Sutherland (1980). Some general conclusions and recommendations may be drawn:

- Text legibility is affected by character height and the distance of the user from the screen. Characters should subtend at least seven (7) minutes of arc of the visual angle of the retina.

- Legibility is affected by brightness, particularly the ratio between text and background. Optimal spacing between letters also depends on brightness. Relative brightness is affected by ambient illumination.

- Headings should be in upper case and the body of the text in a mixture of upper and lower case.

- Character legibility is affected by colour; in general the "brighter" the colour the more legible. The better colours for text are white, yellow, cyan and green.

Presenting "pages" of information on viewdata/teletext type systems demands that the information presented be logically ordered and structured. Whilst electronic systems present the opportunity to use colour, flashing characters, and various graphic devices for emphasis, these may be confusing and distracting if not used judiciously (see above). Champness and de Alberdi (1981) have suggested a set of criteria for assessing text pages, based on experimental research:

- how attractive the pages are judged to be
- how clear they are judged to be
- how useful they are judged to be.

The findings from these experiments, carried out in both England and the U.S.A., suggest that maximum clarity may be attained in page presentation by simply using paragraphs and colour coding the key words for emphasis.

The reading of continuous text from a VDU has been studied experimentally and compared with reading from a book (e.g. Moter et al., 1982). There were no differences between book and VDU in terms of the amount of dizziness experienced in the experiments, in fatigue or eyestrain reported, nor any differences in comprehension scores. However, reading from the VDU screen was 29 per cent slower. This research suggests that continous reading of text from a VDU is certainly possible; however, to gain the same amount of information in the same time, it would be appropriate to synthesize, or summarize VDU presented text.

A recent suggeston as to why reading from a VDU should be relatively slow is that VDU flicker may disrupt saccades (the fast movements of the eye that cause it to flick - without the person's awareness - from place to place when reading) and so slow down reading from a VDU. (Wilkins, A.P.U., Cambridge, personal communication.) Wilkins (1984) has presented evidence that the various aspects of visual discomfort that can sometimes be associated with reading from VDUs have a common physiological basis. Consistent with the psychophysiological view (see chapter 2), there are significant individual differences between people in their susceptibility to the noxious effects, and interactions with the type of task involved and other aspects of the situation. Developments in display technology are likely to result in flicker-free displays and other improvements which will reduce or remove many of the possible physical contributors to visual discomfort in using information systems.

It is certainly feasible in principle to present summary information at the user-system interface, and this need not be second-best compared with paper but could be an improved way of presenting information. As artificial intelligence techniques become more developed in the area of information systems it should become more feasible to tailor the nature of the summary to the needs of the particular task and user. One can imagine, for example, that a system could brief its user about a particular subject by presenting information organised according to a hierarchy, the deeper levels of which would contain more detailed information. The user could move up and down the hierarchy according to his or her state of knowledge and interest in particular aspects of the subject of the briefing.

It may also be possible to improve the way information is presented on a screen, as the work of Pynte and Noizet suggests. Pynte and Noizet (1980) have shown that segmenting the text presented can lead to faster reading. Recent research at Plymouth Polytechnic has shown that randomly segmented sentences can sometimes be read faster than the same sentences presented intact (personal communication).

Voice

The spoken language is generally a less formal version of the written language. It has strengths and weaknesses when compared with text. Voice can add to the verbal message by conveying, for example, irony, emphasis, or in other ways qualifying the meaning of the verbal content using inflection, tone, pitch, and other non-verbal cues. On the other hand, the sequential nature of voice means that it is not as easy to skip backwards and forwards as it is with text. Also, speech rate is generally slower than reading rate, and so it will take longer to listen to a message than to read it.

Considering attentional processing channel capacity, the scope for voice annotation (addition of a voice message to a text document) may be limited. Adding voice annotation to text may well mean that if the user attempts to process both at once to any depth, neither will be processed very well, since both are verbal. On the other hand, adding voice annotation to graphics and images may be very complementary, since words and image combinations do not mutually interfere to anything like the extent that voice and text do (c.f. Mills, 1982). Voice may serve to explain and disambiguate the images and graphics, whilst graphics and images may emphasize the key points in the voice message.

Tables

Tables are an appropriate display format for numerical data, where precise figures are required, although the relative magnitude of imprecise quantities may be better represented graphically. This effect has been demonstrated experimentally by Ikhlef, who found that it is quicker to answer which of a number of activities was the larger when reading from a graph than from a table, but vice-versa when the question was "how much?" (Champness and Ikhlef, 1982). A number of suggestions have been made on formatting tables for VDU display by Sutherland (1980). Empirical evidence is, however, hard to come by. One study compared various formats suggested by Sutherland: Foster and Bruce (1982) compared three colour formats for tables:

- row alternation: had alternate rows in two different colours
- row banding: had blocks of three rows in alternate colours
- column coding: had the columns in different colours.

In addition, inserting a blank line between every three rows of the table was investigated. Two different sorts of question were used of the types:

- What is the value of Y for X ?
- Which X has the value Y ?

Column coding took significantly longer than monochrome or row banding formats; row alternation took significantly longer than row banding. Foster and Bruce suggest that either monochrome or row banding are to be recommended and column coding is disruptive. Inserting a blank row had a neglible effect on performance, but there may be effects with larger, more complex tables.

Graphics

Graphics is an all-encompassing term that covers a number of applications. Perhaps the most important distinction is between the graphical representation of schematized language symbolic relations (e.g. diagrams and flow charts) and the graphical representation of numerical data (graphs).

Diagrams and flow charts. Technical and scientific reports frequently use diagram/flow-chart schemata to present an overview of the structures described in the text. Since one of the problems of presenting large textual documents on electronic systems is the representation of structure, a solution may be to construct and represent such a schema, which could then guide the user's search for specific information within the general structure.

Graphs and charts. Graphs and charts are extremely concise methods of presenting relationships between numerical data points. As a form of imageable representation of numerical relations they are particularly useful for showing trends and projections. It is, perhaps, useful to consider graphs as pictorial analogies for numerical relations with ability to synthesize the product of large amounts of numerical data into imagery. A number of different formats of graph are possible; however, not all forms are equally suitable to represent the particular sort of information that the user wants. A further problem is the lack of standard formats for representing information - for example, whilst the rules for compiling and interpreting a balance sheet are standard, the rules concerning how to use graphs to show similar information are at least ambiguous and probably idiosyncratic (Weidner, 1981; Friend, 1983). This is particularly unfortunate since graphical representation of numerical data is a plausible means of international communication.

Graphs offer a number of opportunities for making full use of the VDU display. Colour is a particularly obvious example. Judicious and consistent use of a colour to code baseline relations against "what if" manipulations and projections is particularly recommended.

A comprehensive review of computer generated graphical display techniques will not be attempted here (see Marcus, 1983, for a useful discussion), but it is worth making some general points:

- Graphical representation is particularly useful for the communication of trends and of relative magnitude (particularly over time).
- Graphs present a rather imprecise distillation of numerical information.
- Graphics packages should be extremely flexible, allowing for the production of different types of graph (see below), also allowing for different types of annotation and varying emphasis.

- The form of graph should be appropriate for the data to be displayed: implicit assumptions underlying the graphical metaphor should be considered.

There are five principal types of chart detailed below. These are appropriate for showing different types of relationships. Since graphs are, in a sense, analogies or "geometrical metaphor" (Bertrand Russell) there are underlying assumptions which need to be considered. The principal types of chart and their implications are as follows.

The Venn Diagram - which is an appropriate form for expressing membership of a category, sets and subsets of categories and overlapping categories. This form of graphical representation is particularly appropriate for categories and subsets which do not have hierarchical organization and for which part of the category remains undefined.

Maps - which are particularly useful for representing geographically distributed information. Maps can be shaded to illustrate the values associated with particular areas. In application areas, map-type graphs are useful: to review characteristics of populations; to determine optimal locations of stores, warehouses, offices, etc., by plotting customers' service needs; in weather mapping; and in assessing environmental consequences of particular actions. A particularly good review of map-type graphs is provided by C.R.S report No. 80-122S.

The pie chart - which, like the bar chart (see below), is particularly useful for showing relative proportions (as slices of a pie). Unlike the bar chart, however, there is something of an assumption that since the pie chart is circular, the whole pie reflects 100% of the universe being described. An implication conveyed by this is that relative proportions are complete descriptions of all the possible combinations, and that all the possible categories are included, which may not be the case - for example, it would be inappropriate to use a pie chart to compare the proportions of tax increases on cigarettes, alcohol and petrol, if there were also tax increases on cars and colour televisions which are not on the chart.

The bar chart (either vertical or horizontal) - which is a frequently used form of graph. Unlike the pie chart, there is no underlying implication that the categories are exhaustive. Bar charts which have discrete bars, not joined to the bars either side imply a separation into discrete parts. When depicting consecutive periods of time it is, therefore, better to join one bar to the next. Vertical bars emphasize the individual magnitudes. Bar charts can also be used like pie charts to imply 100% of the data universe; these bars run the full length of the chart, and are sectioned into component parts. The 100% bars are useful for comparing different breakdowns, such as market share in different years.

Line charts - which are particularly useful for showing changes in value over time. There is a convention that time moves from past to future, and from left-to-right along the horizontal axis, the vertical axis is used for the changing value. Line charts emphasize change and the rate of change. Charts that show a number of lines are difficult to comprehend. As a rule of thumb it is confusing to show more than three lines on any one chart, and preferable to break these apart into multiple charts.

Images

Images are perhaps best considered in terms of their complexity, and the level of detail in the displayed picture. It is not clear that images with full colour and a wealth of detail are always necessary or desirable. Whilst full colour pictures are seen as more attractive and possibly convey more feeling or atmosphere, schematized cartoons have been shown to convey more memorable information. Champness and Ikhlef (1982) showed a full colour fill-in picture of a house or a schematized outline constructed with either Alpha Mosaic images (Prestel type graphics) or Alpha Geometric images (Telidon type graphics), and later asked how many windows the house had. The Alpha Geometric schematized picture was clearly superior; additionally, Alpha Geometric images were seen as more attractive and clearer than the Alpha Mosaic images. It would appear that full colour fill-in graphics may actually inhibit information uptake in some circumstances, and that line drawings may be superior for displaying the meaningful details of the structure. This experimental finding supports the conclusions drawn by Mills (1982) on the comprehension of cartoons, caricatures and pictorial metaphors.

These conclusions and the Champness and Ikhleft experimental results may be explained in terms of schema theory, which suggests that outline drawings and cartoons can be thought of as nearer to the brain's encoding of objects in "canonical form" (Hochberg, 1972), a form of simplified concept. Mills (1981) discusses this further.

A particularly interesting subset of images is iconic symbols. The use of iconic symbols to identify categories of information has received some empirical investigation. Champness and Ikhlef (1982) found that memory for the categories contained in a transportation menu was enhanced when the categories were defined by icons (e.g. an aeroplane, train etc.) rather than words. This experimental result supports the psychological literature (c.f. Bower and Winzenz, 1970) which suggests that the icon must be linked to the content. A further conclusion from the psychological literature (c.f. Bower, 1972) with implications for personal storage and retrieval is that the link between the icon and the material to be retrieved must be under the user's control at the time of filing.

Whilst symbols such as icons may be an attractive alternative in a multi-lingual context, there are difficulties in representing abstract processes - requiring considerable testing and tuning, with large symbol sets requiring considerable user effort.

Animation

The use of animation is generally limited to specific areas: entertainment (e.g. films, home video, games, etc), education, training and presentations. This probably reflects the limitations of current technology, which make animation an expensive and time-consuming mode of presenting information, generally suitable only where repeated presentation of the same animated sequence is envisaged. New technology is likely to transcend both current cost and time limitations. A further difference between the new technologies and the old is that, whilst film and video are linear and sequential, emerging technology (e.g. videodisc) allows rapid access to any part of the stored animated sequence, allowing interactive branching.

Mills (1982) suggests that animated sequences may be most useful in problem solving, since problem-solving is essentially a dynamic process which involves going beyond the information given and restructuring. The use of interactive sequences where the graphic/image sequence depends on choices made by the user allows the consequences of user choice to be represented. Mills also makes a distinction between motion and sequence, and argues that a series of stills allows the perception of sequence, so that the appearance of movement is not always necessary. It is apparent that animated sequences are particularly appropriate for showing cause and effect. The new technologies which allow branching sequences of graphics and images represent an important new opportunity to trace through the consequences that follow decision choices.

There is a difference between the sequential, animated map (movie map) and the traditional static map. Whilst the movie map provides the consequences (in images) of turning right at an intersection, providing visual feedback, the traditional map is still clearly superior in providing answers to questions like: How far is it from here to X? In what direction is X? How do I get to X?

In summary, new technology provides an opportunity to show in images/graphics, the consequences (dynamic state changes) of decision choice. The sequential nature of animation is particularly appropriate for representing causal relationships.

Animation is a "species of information" that in principle can thrive much better in the computer-based environment of the emerging office than in the paper-based environment of the past, because of the ease of producing animation at low cost. In order to survive, however, it will need to compete with other "species" in terms of its effectiveness for presenting information in a way well suited to office work. This is equally true of the other "species" considered above. It will certainly be the case that the mix of "species" seen today will change as electronic office systems become more widespread, and the possibilities for optimising the presentation of information become more evident.

TRENDS IN OPTIMISING THE PRESENTATION OF INFORMATION: MIXING FORMS OF PRESENTATION

New technology will provide the opportunity to mix forms of presentation with much greater flexibility and at far lower cost than is possible at present. The key need that arises from a human factors viewpoint is to enable the user to integrate the various forms easily. The design of an efficient and consistent user-system interface is very much a problem of combining the various manipulations under a consistent schema.

There is no reason in principle why a sophisticated interface should not be able to recommend to the user optimal formats for the information to be represented. However, those recommendations should be grounded in sufficient human factors research. One obvious combination of forms illustrates this point. This is the combination of graphics/images and text. What is the best way of formatting this combination? Ellis & Miller (1981) found that, for advertisements, right-handed people prefer the picture to the left of the text, whilst left handers express no particular preference. Whether or not this result generalizes to other text/graphic/image combinations, or other situations, is an empirical question, but it illustrates the need to research even the "obvious" situations carefully.

Research on effective presentation of information in the paper-based environment may be a useful starting point (e.g. Easterby and Zwaga, 1984; Wright, 1977), but research is needed in order to see to what extent the findings from the paper-based environment apply to the electronic environment, and to explore the novel features of the electronic environment (e.g. the possibility of using animation in various ways).

AREAS WHERE RESEARCH IS NEEDED

Office workers in the paper-based environment have been restricted in how they could present and communicate information. The chief form used has been text, tables of numbers, and simple diagrams and charts - largely because of the practicalities involved in using paper rather than the inherent effectiveness of these forms of communication. The use of 35mm slides, of tape-slide presentations, and of video has been restricted to special circumstances (e.g. client presentations, presentations to senior management, conference papers), and the integrated use of several media at once has hardly been used at all.

All this can change in the integrated electronic office where, in technical terms at least, it will be possible to send video and voice as easily as text. In order to capitalise upon this technical potential to the full, it is necessary to research:

- how different media and combinations of media can be used most effectively to communicate facts, concepts, imaginative ideas, strategic plans, and so forth;

- how best to present such a multimedia environment to the user, so that (s)he can create and deal with multimedia communications as easily and as effectively as possible.

One can imagine in the multimedia electronic environment that one will be creating, sending and receiving fewer memos and reports of a conventional sort and more multimedia packages that might look more like mini television documentaries than conventional "papers". Voice annotation of text is already commonplace, and the advent of video and optical discs means that a marked increase in the use of still and moving pictures is just around the corner. The effective use of these new capabilities in human communication depends upon researching the psychology of multimedia representation and manipulation.

The research needs to be related to other aspects of the broader problem. A particularly important aspect of this is the relationship to information storage and retrieval. Even today, graphics packages of various sorts are becoming widespread for creating 35mm slides and for other purposes. One of the significant weaknesses of these packages is in the area of storage and retrieval of the images created. Normally this depends upon labelling the images with keywords, and using these labels to retrieve images. Even for relatively small numbers of such images this becomes cumbersome and awkward. And this is when only one medium is involved. For the very large number of multimedia items envisaged in a typical electronic office environment (perhaps thousands per office worker), such a crude system of storage and retrieval will be inadequate and more sophisticated user interface techniques will have to be developed.

This links in turn to the need to consider hierarchies of information (discussed above), and the need to present only that information which is relevant at an appropriate level of detail matched to the needs of the particular user in a particular situation. This requires research that addresses the joint problems of optimal presentation, optimal accessing of relevant information, and optimal use of artificial intelligence within the system.

SUGGESTED FURTHER READING

Easterby, R. & Zwaga, H. (1984)
Information design: the design and evaluation of signs and printed material. Chichester: John Wiley & Sons.

Marcus, A. (1983)
InterGraphics '83: tutorial sessions A4. World Computer Graphics Association, Inc., 2033 M Street N.W. Suite 399, Washington, D.C. 20036, U.S.A.

Wright, P. (1977)
Presenting technical information: a survey of research findings. International Science, 6, 93-134.

THE NEXT CHAPTER

This concludes the individual topics considered in the Preparatory Study. In the next chapter, we review the key areas of research identified.

CHAPTER 6:

KEY AREAS FOR RESEARCH

INTRODUCTION

The preceeding chapters have outlined key aspects of the human factors of office systems. Each of them provides a starting point for years of human factors research effort. It has been estimated that something of the order of 350 person-years of research is needed in order to cover the areas at all adequately. What are the priorities within this field? The authors of the Preparatory Study on which this book is based were asked to identify a relatively small number of topics where research should be encouraged under the ESPRIT programme. This chapter presents an overview of the key research areas that were identified. They cover five broad topic areas:

1 definition of the problem
   - models of user-system interaction
   - the psychophysiological context
   - the organisational context
   - functional analysis and definition of new services
   - evaluation

2 species of interaction
- human-machine cognitive compatibility
- optimal building blocks
- dialogue design methodology

3 the user's model of the system
- design guidelines
- training and guidance
- adaptive interfaces
- office system architecture model

4 the representation of information
- system control
- substantive information
- knowledge management

5 broader concerns
- links between industry and academia
- links between member states

DEFINITION OF THE PROBLEM

Models of User-System Interaction

User-system interaction in the context of electronic office systems is concerned with the processing of information. The electronic office system itself is based on information processing technology; the human can be regarded as an information processing system; and the combination of the two makes an information processing system that is a hybrid of a biological and electronic system.

Models of this type of hybrid information processing system are essential if one is to be able to understand, talk meaningfully about, and optimise, user-system interaction. Pre-models exist in two main disciplines: cognitive psychology (concerned with the human), and artificial intelligence (concerned with the electronic system). Research should be encouraged in both of these areas, and in particular research should be encouraged which draws on both and brings the two together to develop a new class of model that is concerned neither with the human in isolation nor the electronic system in isolation but with a hybrid information processing system incorporating both.

The Psychophysiological Context

The Human Factors view of electronic office systems starts from the assumption that such systems are intended to serve and to be used by humans, not the other way around. The Psychophysiological view within Human Factors contends that the human's interactions with electronic office systems need to be considered:

a. at different levels

b. within the context of the human's life as a whole - both the work situation as whole, and other aspects of the person's life.

The different levels at which user-system interaction needs to be considered include the

- behavioural (observable behaviour)
- cognitive (underlying information processing)
- affective (feelings, emotions)
- physiological (including physiological stress reactions).

Optimal design of the user-system interface requires attention to all these levels. Research should be encouraged to develop a better understanding of what characteristics of the user-system interface are particularly important, and how, in affecting key psychophysiological aspects of user-system information processing. These key aspects include:

- psychophysiological arousal
- mental load
- psychophysiological stress.

Special attention should be given to the following topics:

- hardware ergonomics
- design of the dialogue
- machine-pacing and self-pacing
- requirements for vigilance
- individual differences in human responses to working with electronic systems
- the meaning of work in the office of the future.

Appropriate research methods need to be developed for dealing with user-system interaction at the different levels involved. Research should be encouraged to apply methods used in psychophysiological work generally to the particular context of user-system interaction. These methods use a variety of different types of data, spanning the different levels involved. These include:

- verbal reports (e.g. interviews, questionnaires)
- video analysis
- physiological measures of various sorts, e.g
  - eye movements
  - pupil reactions
  - heart rate

- event-related brain potentials
- background EEG
- catecholamine levels.

These various measures can be used to provide information about different aspects of user-system interaction. For example, eye movements can indicate where the user is looking, verbal report can indicate why the user is looking there, and some of the other physiological measures can provide information about the level of stress the user is under. This is just an illustrative, partial example, and research is needed to refine the various techniques involved in order that they can be used to greatest effect.

The Organisational Context

The Psychophysiological Human Factors view emphasises that user-system interaction does not take place "in a vacuum" but in a very real context - the organisational context, and the more general life context. Research is needed on both of these, but the former is appropriate under ESPRIT and the latter perhaps less so.

Research on the organisational context needs to:

- segment the population of potential users of office systems according to their needs, and to define the main categories of office systems that will be required in order to meet those needs

- identify the key services which office systems in each major category need to provide

- develop models of organisations that are best suited to the introduction and use of electronic office technology

- develop methods of organisation development that are geared specifically to the problem of introducing electronic office technology in the best possible way within an optimal organisational framework.

In segmenting the population of users, the need is to define categories in terms that relate directly to the kinds of things the people concerned will need to do with the new systems. This means that the research must take account of changes that the movement towards an electronic environment can be expected to bring about. The kinds of things that a manager, a scientific professional, a secretary, and a clerical worker will do in an electronic office environment can be expected to be different from what they do in the paper-based environment of today. Consequently, traditional ways of categorising office workers (e.g. manager, secretary, clerical worker) may not be as useful as some new scheme that cuts across the traditional distinctions.

In identifying the key services which need to be provided, the research needs to take account of likely changes in organisational goals and sub-goals over the next five to ten years. It is unlikely that the mix of business will remain constant; organisations will need to adapt to a changing economic and social environment. There are also trends in the pressures on organisations to perform better or differently within existing goal-frameworks - for example, by delivering their services faster, meeting higher standards, providing more detailed and more frequent information about their activities to third parties including government.

In developing models of organisations that are best suited to the introduction and use of electronic office technology, account needs to be taken of possible and likely impacts that electronic office systems can reasonably be expected to have. Some of the key issues here relate, for example, to:

- decreasing dependency between the functional and the physical office, e.g. possibilities for shared offices or offices rented by the hour or day, working from home, neighbourhood work centres, communication with the office from hotel, client location and car

- decreasing dependency on particular time slots, e.g. facilitating part-time working, international business transactions, more flexible structuring to the day and week

- easier access to a wider range of resources at a company, national and international level, e.g. use of electronic networks to access databases throughout Europe

- less costly and easier access to expert advice, both through artificially intelligent "expert systems" as such and through various information services

- greater autonomy for the professional and others in planning the working day

- more possibilities for skill enrichment through the use of electronic tutoring systems of various sorts

- greater possibilities for decentralisation of work

- greater possibilities for democratic organisational decision-making

- greater possibilities for control of the formal organisation from the centre, but, equally, greater difficulty in exerting central control of the informal organisation.

In developing methods of organisation development that are geared specifically to the problem of introducing electronic office technology in the best possible way, it will be at least as important as in any other area of organisation development, and more important than in many, to take a total "systems" approach. The opportunities and hazards associated with the introduction of electronic office systems extend throughout all aspects of an organisation, have implications at every level, and potentially reach into every organisational detail. The total effects on any given organisation cannot all be predicted at the outset - the whole is greater than the sum of its parts, and there will be "emergent properties" of the new organisational system in every case that could not be foreseen. No one person and no one machine will understand the system in its totality. The potential "culture shock" of moving into a new kind of working environment could be enormous, and is matched by the enormous benefits that can be gained if the transition is handled effectively.

Functional Analysis

In order to achieve an optimal transition to an electronic office environment, a key requirement from the systems design point of view is an adequate "functional analysis" of a representative range of organisation types. The functional analysis needs to develop, for each major type of organisation, a model that identifies the key goals and sub-goals of the organisation type, and links these to a defined set of lower-level functions that need to be performed successfully in order for the organisation to achieve its goals and sub-goals. These major functions in turn need to be analysed in terms of the particular information processing and communications activities they require, and they need to be allocated to humans or machines. The allocation is as much a socio-political question as one of any "objective logic" and so this aspect of the functional analysis needs to draw heavily on the results of the research into the organisational context, above.

The view being advocated here recognises that existing office activities reflect an interaction between today's office systems and more fundamental needs. For example, a particular telephone call may reflect an interaction between an available technology (standard voice telephone) and a need to interact in real time with another person urgently. If there is also a need to exchange papers, that would normally have to be done some other way using today's technology (eg. facsimile). If a strong link could be identified between two types of activity (eg. talking and exchanging papers) this might be taken as an indication of an opportunity for a new service which could support both activities simultaneously.

Directly observable activities of this sort reflect higher-level needs such as the need to exchange information, to find relevant information from external sources, to produce appropriate documentation, and so on. These in turn reflect still higher-level business functions related to marketing, accounting, personnel and so forth.

A language and appropriate theoretical models are needed to describe the linkages between activities and needs at different levels, and the "information circuits" that are needed to support the necessary organizational communications. The models need to take account of relevant differences between different types of organisation and between different countries.

There is a need for an international study of office requirements in relation to information technology. This study needs to examine the functional aspects of office activities in terms of information handling and communications, and to relate these to business functions and information circuits.

The study should aim to develop a theoretical understanding of the potential for office automation. It could usefully incorporate the knowledge gained into a computer-based model of office activities and functions.

A major output from the functional analysis needs to be a clear definition and high-level specification of each of a number of key "electronic services" and how these interrelate. Some of these can reasonably be expected to correspond roughly to existing concepts such as word processing, database access, spreadsheet facilities, and so forth. New concepts should also emerge, some of which may cut across existing distinctions. Even more important, the research should lead to the definition and specification of "higher-level services" which incorporate elements of the kinds of "application packages" we see today as well as new concepts, and which do more for the user than any single one of today's "applications".

Filing and retrieval of unstructured information. One of the key elements that needs to be researched in developing these electronic services is the ability to handle unstructured information. This is a distinguishing characteristic of many office environments where new systems are aimed. The filing and retrieval of such information is a key aspect of this. It has not been handled very well from a human factors point of view by existing electronic systems and is one key example of an area where research is needed in order to develop new electronic services in a way that is well-suited to the nature of the office work involved.

An example of a relatively unstructured office is that of the professional. In such an office, there is typically a flexible mix of media used (paper, dictation, voice annotation, graphics, video) and the types of items handled (books, journals, letters, memos, comments, etc). The retrieval of unstructured information in such an office has a number of special characteristics with which existing electronic systems typically do not deal very well, and with which future systems must. These include the following:

- items may have many different areas of relevance
- items may have no current relevance but may be required in the future
- current needs may require a different structure from the filing system that exists
- multi-media information may be difficult to store as a unique entity because of the characteristics of the media and filing methods.

Research is needed to develop an understanding of the psychology of unstructured information retrieval and to apply that understanding to the problem of designing an electronic environment that is compatible with human cognitive processes. Similar needs apply to other key services, which need to be identified systematically as part of the functional analysis research.

Use of artificial intelligence. The higher-level services are likely to incorporate artificial intelligence, both as intelligence that is directly available to the user (e.g. knowledge bases) and intelligence that is hidden in the system and is used to operate and manage the work that is done, from the user's point of view, "behind the scenes" (e.g. identification of appropriate databases and interpretation of the user's requirements into a form that can be used to access the databases).

Office system architecture model. Complementing the functional analysis research, and being its technical counterpart, an office system architecture model is needed to provide a conceptual framework or plan for a system. Without such a model, mere communication facilities, even those on a file transfer level, would lead to isolated and heterogeneous system solutions. This goes beyond the purely technical. Compatibility of different systems will be needed at the user interface as well as "behind the scenes" or the benefits of the technical compatibility will be lost due to confusion in the user's model of the system.

Evaluation

The Human Factors approach to evaluation advocated here contends that electronic office systems need to be evaluated in terms of how well they address the total problem as described above and in Chapter 2, not just one particular aspect of it.

Evaluation therefore needs to address

- the behavioural, cognitive, affective and physiological aspects of user-system interaction, identified and defined within the psychophysiological framework - this depends upon adequate models of user-system interaction, in order to be able to define the appropriate measures for evaluation

- the organisational context, including individual and group effectiveness in contributing to the achievement of organisational goals, as well as socio-economic factors relating to the individual, the work group, and the wider context - this depends upon an adequate definition and specification of the high-level services to be provided, and their lower-level components.

Research on evaluation within the ESPRIT Programme could usefully include the tailoring of appropriate evaluation methods developed in other areas of human factors to the special case of electronic office systems. This aspect of the work could include development of new techniques. Particular attention could be given to:

- methods of videotape analysis for evaluation at the behavioural level

- methods of applying cognitive psychology theory to the evaluation of human-machine cognitive compatibility

- the development of subjective assessment techniques and other methods for evaluation of users' affective (emotional) responses to working with electronic systems

- the application and refinement of techniques based on recording of eye movements, heart rate, background EEG, evoked potentials, and other physiological indices of user-system interaction.

Useful as such research is, what is even more important is the development of an overall methodology - a complete structural and procedural research environment that is optimal for researching new electronic office systems. The need for such a methodology comes from the need to deal with the complexity of the problem on its own terms, rather than solving simpler problems that are more amenable to control and quantification but which do not contribute as fully to the development of new and better concepts in electronic office systems. The technology of electronic office systems is evolving so rapidly that it is outstripping our understanding of the human aspects. Human Factors needs to adapt to this situation. Traditional methods need to be developed further, and in many cases supplemented by new and more appropriate methods of research.

CAFE OF EVE. Alluding to the first major knowledge explosion in which an apple figured prominently, in the Garden of Eden, and consistent with the promise of a knowledge explosion that is associated with the development of new electronic systems, the term CAFE OF EVE has been proposed for the new methodology that is required (Gale, Scane and colleagues, Southampton University).

The CAFE OF EVE would be a Controlled, Adaptive, Flexible, Experimental Office of the Future, in an Ecologically Valid Environment. It would combine the most appropriate features of controlled laboratory experimental methods with the most appropriate features of field research methods, and add some new, emergent properties.

The CAFE OF EVE would provide an environment in which evaluation of electronic office systems could be conducted at all levels, and at all stages of the design process. It would therefore provide a total answer to the problem, and not just a partial answer to some particular aspect of it. In addition, it would provide a European Showcase in which new and effective concepts in electronic office systems could been demonstrated in a real working environment.

The CAFE OF EVE would be set up in an operating section of a company, as a real-life functional simulation of the Office of the Future. The experimental office complex would be equipped with operational electronic office systems at various stages of development from early working prototypes through to finished products. It would also be fully equipped with state-of-the-art human factors equipment for research purposes, including detailed monitoring of the day to day functioning of the office complex, which would provide for an in-depth, longitudinal functional analysis of the requirements which electronic office systems need to meet. The experimental office complex would therefore be a test-bed for new ideas, and a real organisation "under the microscope" for the purposes of functional analysis.

Attached to the office complex, as an integral part of the research environment, would be a suite of rooms where controlled laboratory experiments could be conducted. This would include facilities for rapidly designing new user interface concepts and mocking them up in interactive hardware and software. This would be staffed by a team of psychologists, systems analysts, programmers, and research assistants.

The subjects in the controlled experiments would be the employees in the office complex, and the concepts developed in the experiments would be prototyped in the real working environment in the office complex itself. The results of the prototyping, together with the ongoing functional analysis that would be conducted in the real working areas, would feed back to contribute to the design of further experiments.

The employees within the CAFE OF EVE would be office workers recruited in the normal fashion, except that their job description would include as a specific aspect of their work their role in the research programme. As participants in the research programme they would be both "researchers" and "guinea pigs" (subjects). They would be expected to discharge their normal work functions as part of the substantive business of the organisation, and as a recognised part of their work, they would also offer suggestions in relation to their work experience and the opportunities for information technology, join in the research programme, and act as experimental subjects. Typically, in conventional research environments, there is a status gap between the researchers and those who are researched, and a difference in aims. The CAFE OF EVE would incorporate the notions of partnership and sharing of common goals between the researchers and the office workers, facilitating an open dialogue between the two. This would be a novel feature of the research environment, and requires research in its own right to develop the necessary techniques for data collection and analysis, building upon techniques which have been established in other contexts.

The CAFE OF EVE as conceived of by Gale, Scane and colleagues at Southampton University is a special human factors research and development environment which takes the most appropriate features of the normal working environment and of the traditional controlled experiment and builds upon them to create a new kind of research environment designed to meet the special requirements of human factors research into advanced office systems.

SPECIES OF INTERACTION

Human-Machine Cognitive Compatibility

The various "species of interaction" that emerging technology makes possible differ in their attentional, memory, and other cognitive demands they make on the user. They differ in how apprpriate they are for different kinds of user at different levels of familiarity with the system, and in different task contexts. Wherever a particular species is appropriate in principle, an indefinitely large number of particular dialogues can be constructed - most of which will be sub-optimal in terms of how well they "mesh in" with the way the human is designed.

The human is designed to be very adaptive to its environment and has shown itself capable of learning to cope fairly well even with poorly designed human-machine dialogues. Even so, the onus is on the designer of electronic office systems to try and optimise their design as far as possible, so that the design fits in well rather than poorly with the way the human is built. In terms of the flow of communication between the user and the office system, this means designing the dialogue to be compatible with the cognitive make-up of the human.

In designing for cognitive compatibility, it is not necessary to start from "square one". A great deal of research, amounting to thousands of person-years, has already been done on the cognitive psychology of the human being. This research has been done in the academic institutions over the last twenty-five years or so and should not now be overlooked.

Research effort could usefully be focussed on three main areas:

1. There is a need to review what has been done and identify what is of most relevance to human-machine interaction in the context of electronic office systems. Areas which are particularly likely to be fruitful include research that has been done on the cognitive processes invloved in:
    - acquiring new skills
    - thinking and reasoning
    - developing and using mental models
    - semantic and episodic memory
    - language (psycholinguistics).

2. Where relevant and applicable knowledge exists, research should be encouraged on developing methods for "packaging" that knowledge in a form that can be used by designers of office systems without them having to become cognitive psychologists themselves. This could possibly make use of techniques developed under the "expert systems" rubric, but other possibilities should be examined as well, and the research should not be constrained to fit within the typical "expert systems" mould.

3. Much of the mainstream cognitive psychology research done so far may be of only indirect relevance to the problem of user-system interaction. There is a need to review what has

been done and identify gaps where more "pure" research could usefully be encouraged in order to facilitate the further development of mainstream cognitive psychology in directions that are going to be fruitful for Information Technology.

Optimal Building Blocks

Two key needs, amongst others, in writing software to support user-system interaction are:

- to design the dialogue (including screen layouts, sequences of interactions, and associated aspects of user-system interaction) optimally from the human factors point of view

- to avoid unnecessary rewriting of code - to avoid "reinventing the wheel" for each new product.

One practical way of helping to meet both of these needs is to provide standard code and specifications for code in the form of "building blocks" that have been optimised in terms of their human factors. These building blocks would provide a means of incorporating the results of human factors research into the design of products in a very practical way. They would therefore be an important contribution to standards for user interface design.

The building blocks would be "micro-dialogues" that could be fitted together to build up more complex sequences of user-system dialogue. They would be, for example, optimal designs for particular kinds of menus, for particular aspects of windowing, and for particular instances of speech command. They would be the elements within the various "species of interaction".

The building blocks should not be defined arbitrarily but should be based on a careful psychological analysis of what the basic "units of behaviour" are within an electronic office environment.

The building blocks should be validated in controlled human factors experiments and in simulated "real office" situations.

Dialogue Design Methodology

The availability of standard, optimal building blocks would go a considerable way towards facilitating the dialogue design for a new product. However, the building blocks would still have to be organised into an overall design, and the building blocks themselves need to be designed. For both of these reasons, there is a need to develop a methodology for dialogue design that covers three main areas:

1. A formal Human Factors Language for specifying a dialogue design. This language needs to incorporate human factors concepts at an appropriate level of detail to support communication between the human factors specialists and the team doing the coding. The language should also be sufficiently detailed to allow automated or manual human factors evaluation of the proposed dialogue to be conducted. The language needs to go beyond existing design languages to incorporate human factors concepts.

2. Automated methods for evaluating dialogue design specifications produced by the Human Factors Language. This relates to the "packaging" of cognitive psychology referred to above. The aim would be to develop automated methods which the designer could use to apply what is known about human cognitive psychology in order to evaluate proposed dialogue designs, which could then be improved by making suitable modifications. The ability to apply the evaluation

methods to written specifications rather than actual software would be economical in terms of time and effort.

3. A package to allow the designer to rapidly produce an interactive mock-up of the proposed dialogue design (complete with actual screen layouts, and so forth). This would mean that once specifications have been optimised as far as possible on the basis of (1) and (2) above they could be evaluated in more detail in controlled experiments, using interactive mock-ups.

THE USER'S MODEL OF THE SYSTEM

Design Guidelines

Guidelines concerning how to facilitate the development by the user of an optimal model of the system, and how to facilitate use of that model by the user, need to be established.

This is part of a broader area relating to the development and publication of human factors design guidelines in general. Research is needed on:

- the most appropriate role for guidelines in the provision of human factors support to designers of electronic office systems

- alternatives, and complements to guidelines as such

- how to present guidelines, where they are an appropriate way of providing human factors support, so they are presented in the most useful and acceptable form - including research on alternative ways of automating guidelines

. a methodology for developing guidelines systematically across national and industry boundaries, for maintaining and continuously updating a database of these guidelines, for exercising quality control in terms of their validity, for facilitating and monitoring their progress towards standards where this is appropriate, and for making them available to designers of office systems in all the Member States.

Training and Guidance

The acceptance of an electronic office product depends critically upon the ease with which new users can learn an appropriate model of the product, and can receive appropriate help when required. New users of electronic office systems often do not wish to go on lengthy training courses in order to be able to use the systems, and experience also suggests that they seldom make much use of conventional user manuals.

Research is needed to develop ways of incorporating learning and help techniques within the systems themselves, so that the system itself provides the user with the support needed during the initial learning phase and subsequently when help is required to recover from errors, resolve minor uncertainties, or to learn more advanced features.

Techniques of on-line training borrowed from the area of computer-assisted learning and other areas have not been fully evaluated for their applicability to office products; also, the tutorials are usually seen as separate from the real work the user will be doing with the product later, and there is a need to develop techniques which are a more intrinsic part of using the product - bringing the concepts of "training" and "help" rather closer together than they usually are today.

Adaptive Interfaces

The discussion of the user's model of the system, in Chapter 4, emphasises that there is no single, true model of any environment, but only a set of possible models any one of which may be optimal for certain purposes at particular points in time. It follows that the user may not learn a single model of the system, and it may in fact be desirable for the user to switch between different models in learning to become more expert with the system or in using the system for different purposes.

Research is needed on techniques for presenting the same electronic system in different ways according to the particular user and the task in hand. The role of metaphor and analogy is particularly worth exploring, as is research on the schemas and scripts that people take with them from the paper-based office to the electronic office. Research on how schemas and scripts can become modified and extended to include new elements also needs to be researched in the context of office systems.

Office System Architecture Model

The need for an office system architecture model was discussed above as a technical complement to the functional analysis research. In terms of the user's model of the system, the office system architecture model would facilitate compatibility between different office systems in terms of the way they would be presented to the user, and so facilitate the development by the user of a consistent model of the overall system.

One possible approach in principle to facilitating consistency in the user's model might be a standardisation of at least some of the objects and functions involved in office automation, in terms of the way they are defined and represented at the user interface. There is indeed a discernible trend towards de facto standards in some areas. For example, where the "desktop metaphor" is used, different products tend to use similar icons to represent similar objects and functions (e.g. quasi-standard ways of representing the "in-tray", "out-tray", "folders", and so forth). The same applies in some other areas as well - for example, one can recognise a "spreadsheet" when one sees one because they tend to adopt a fairly standard form of presentation to the user.

These quasi-standards that are beginning to emerge are not rigidly defined, and it may be premature to try and define rigid standards in any but a few areas - and undesirable until appropriate research has been done. Another, less ambitious approach, could be to elaborate an office system architecture model which would not claim to be the basis for a rigid standardisation but which could serve as a guideline for individual system development efforts and comparison of individual systems at various technical levels.

The key activity should be the detailed elaboration of a well structured and technically-oriented architecture model. A system model may be called an architecture model if it identifies not only the services offered on the topmost (directly observable) level but also reveals some of the internal structure of the system. To be well-structured it needs to define horizontal structure (in layers) and vertical structure (in self-contained object categories and related functional categories).

The development of such a model means identifying the constitutent structure and identifying which functions may be used to perform which operations. Primitive objects and functions need to be described, and their relationship to the operations and higher-level functions in the model. Precisely how a function is implemented need not be described in the model, but only which service it will offer to a user (which may be a human or another function), and which other services it is allowed to use. It is at this level that the work on developing the model links most directly to the outputs from the functional analysis research.

SPECIES OF INFORMATION

System Control

An increasing variety of possiblities exists for the communication of control information between the user and the electronic system, as discussed in Chapter 2 on "species of interaction". There is a need for research on methods for optimising the dialogue designs developed around these different species, and this has been discussed above in terms of the provision of design guidelines, the application of cognitive psychology, the development of tools for mocking-up proposed designs in interactive hardware and software, and so forth.

Standards. It has also been noted above, in discussion of the need for an office system architecture model, that there is a trend towards quasi-standardisation in some areas. Research is needed to identify these areas more precisely, and other areas where standards for the representation of icons, design of windows, design of menus, and so forth, could be practicable. Appropriate experimental and other research then needs to be done to develop standards that are optimal from the Human Factors point of view. This relates to the need for optimal building blocks, discussed above. Moves towards premature rigid standardisation in the absence of adequate human factors research need to be resisted as they would be much more likely to have deleterious rather than beneficial effects in terms of the human factors of the user-system interface. For essentially the same reason, appropriate research needs to be strongly encouraged so that it can feed into the design of products before de facto standards become established.

Substantive Information

Office workers in the paper-based environment have been restricted in how they could represent and communicate the substantive information of interest to them in their work. The chief form used has been text, tables of numbers, and simple diagrams and charts - largely because of the practicalities involved in using paper rather than the effectiveness of these forms of communication. The use of 35mm slides, of tape-slide presentations, and of video has been restricted to special purposes (e.g. client presentations, presentations to senior management, conference papers), and the integrated use of several media at once has hardly been used at all.

All this can change in the integrated electronic office where, in technical terms at least, it will be possible to send video and voice as easily as text. In order to capitalise upon this technical potential to the full, it is necessary to research:

- how different media and combinations of media can be used most effectively to communicate facts, concepts, imaginative ideas, strategic plans, and so forth

- how best to present such a multimedia environment to the user, so that (s)he can create and deal with multimedia communications as easily and as effectively as possible.

One can imagine in the multimedia electronic environment that one will be creating, sending and receiving fewer memos and reports of a conventional sort and more multimedia packages that might look more like mini television documentaries than conventional "papers". Voice annotation of text is already commonplace, image-capturing and graphics packages of various sorts are becoming widespread, and the advent of video and optical discs means that a marked increase in the use of still and moving pictures is just around the corner. The effective use of these new capabilities in human communication depends upon researching the psychology of multimedia representation and manipulation.

The research needs to be related to other aspects of the broader problem. A particularly important aspect of this is the relationship to information storage and retrieval. Even today, graphics packages of various sorts are becoming widespread for creating 35mm slides and for other purposes. One of the significant weaknesses of these packages is in the area of storage and retrieval of the images created. Normally this depends upon labelling the images with keywords, and using these labels to retrieve images. Even for relatively small numbers of such images this becomes cumbersome and awkward. And this is when only one medium is involved. For the very large number of multimedia items envisaged in a typical electronic office environment (perhaps thousands per office worker), such a crude system of storage and retrieval will be inadequate and more sophisticated user interface techniques will have to be developed.

Multimedia workstation. Research is needed on both the technical integration of different media within a workstation, and the functional, psychological integration at the user interface. Technical integration alone is not sufficient to ensure the success of a system. The potential of the underlying technology will be quite literally wasted in practice unless the different media are brought together appropriately at the user interface and can be manipulated easily and effectively by the user.

This includes the need to consider what kinds of objects and functions should be offered by the workstation, the suitability of different approaches to the user-system dialogue, the ergonomic suitability of various multi-media hardware devices for specific user tasks, and the adaptability of the workstation to the overall office environment. The human factors of these aspects of the design need to be considered within a broader framework which takes account of technical factors and economic considerations.

The evaluation needs to be based both on controlled human factors experiments and on evaluation of prototype workstations in a real world office environment. The CAFE OF EVE described above in relation to evaluation generally would be an appropriate research environment.

Knowledge Management

A major problem that managers and professionals in the office have experienced for many years already is the paradox that on the one hand they are deluged by papers, documents, computer printout and other "information", whilst on the other hand they experience difficulty in obtaining the key items they really need, presented in a form that they would find most useful. This problem could become worse as the amount of information increases (and electronic systems encourage this) and the number of "knowledge workers" increases, unless it is taken specifically into account in the design of electronic environments. There is a need for electronic office systems that will support the delivery of "knowledge" rather than "raw information" to the end user.

There are actually two aspects to this problem. First, there is a need to convert raw information into knowledge. Secondly -

concerning knowledge that is already in the form of knowledge (eg. in experts' "heads") - there is a need to capture that knowledge electronically.

The aim of this topic area would be to develop methods for supporting the conversion of raw information into knowledge, for capturing knowledge efficiently from people who have it (eg. experts), and for presenting that knowledge to users in the most effective way.

Two related additional areas where research is needed to optimise the application of artificial intelligence to office systems are in relation to:

- learning systems, where the electronic office system can adapt to the needs of the particular user
- information filtering, where the system applies a coarse filter to the information being delivered to users in order to maximise relevance and minimise information overload.

These areas all require a cooperative effort from psychologists (to analyse the user aspects) and specialists in artifical intelligence (to develop and apply appropriate machine models).

BROADER CONCERNS

Links Between Industry and Academia

Europe seems to have been lagging behind the USA and Japan in the research and development of new Information Technology. At the same time, Europe is a large land and population mass, and rich in industrial and academic enterprises. It seems reasonable to suppose that Europe could improve its position if it could develop optimal ways of harnessing the knowledge and expertise available in industry and academia. Forming the right sort of linkages between these two sorts of enterprises could be an important element in this.

This is as important in the Human Factors area as any other, and perhaps more so. The developments in technology have been occurring faster than in Human Factors, and have begun significantly to outstrip our scientific understanding of the psychology of the user, and related human factors. There is an urgent need to redress this imbalance if technology is to develop in a way best suited to serve the needs of users in industry and elsewhere.

There is a need to identify the particular areas where improvements in communication, information exchange and development of working relationships would be most likely to be fruitful, and the relative benefit of improvements in this area compared with other factors that may also be important in influencing the development of Information Technology. The analysis should include comparisons with non-European countries to identify any strategies that might be used profitably elsewhere and that could perhaps provide models for Europe.

The notion that the two systems (ie. universities and industry) should communicate with each other presupposes the notion that the systems themselves have adequate internal communications. In regard to Information Technology, this remains to be demonstrated, and the research could usefully examine ways in which internal communications could be facilitated.

It is likely that the considerations relating to possible commercial exploitation could often inhibit dissemination of information. This may sometimes inhibit communication between the universities and industry.

Whilst improvement in information exchange between universities and industry could be a necessary condition for improvement, it is doubtful whether it would be sufficient. Most problems on this scale are complex and require a multi-faceted approach to their solution. Research on this would need to be coordinated with other initiatives in the same area.

Following the acquisition of data on the existing situation, a multivariate model should be constructed to include a set of variables describing links between universities and industry in relation to other key variables. This involves the acquisition of data regarding existing practices. This might include, amongst other things, data on:

- science parks
- advisory research units
- joint projects with Research Councils
- central government department initiatives
- staff exchanges
- student industrial placements
- industry-sponsored bursaries for undergraduates and postgraduates
- special conferences and seminars.

The case study method could be used to sample exemplars of each of the existing kinds of links set out above to determine their success.

It is possible that false perceptions exist in both industry and academia as to the nature of benefits and disadvantages which might accrue through increased communication. Survey and interview techniques could be employed to explore these mutual perceptions, with a view to devising remedial programmes of reeducation as well as to identify types of initiatives that can usefully be built upon.

On the basis of information acquired from the above, a formal model should be constructed of the nature of existing modes of information exchange between universities and industry. Any initiatives proposed for improvements would need to focus on the elements within this formal model. The various modes of linkage between universities and industry may load on different aspects of information exchange not only in terms of type of exchange but in terms of process and changes over time.

It would be important for the research to recognise that the academic institutions serve a number of roles within the community. Recently in the U.K. especially there has been considerable discussion of the notion of "relevance" and the alleged shortcomings of the academic institutions to contribute sufficiently to industrial success. The nature of the relationship between "pure" and "applied" research is very complex, and some would even question the validity of the distinction. There is a danger that in relation to Information Technology, studies of information exchange between universities and industry might focus too much on exchange of technological information. It may well be that the exchange would benefit from a variety of inputs, ranging through technology, basic science, and the social sciences, including management and business economics. Both industry and universities are made up of a variety of constituent parts. It is essential that information be exchanged at several functional points and several functional levels within both organisational frameworks.

Links Between Member States

A closely related question is how to facilitate appropriate

communication among the Member States. One of the significant problems which faces Europe in this respect - as distinct from the U.S.A., for example - is the need to cross language barriers.

Interlingual communication. Interlingual communication is important for collaboration generally within the European Community. Even within a given country, interlingual communication can be important. The Commission of the European Communities itself is an excellent example of an organisation where this is a significant feature of its work. It will be important for Europe to establish the necessary communication links, and to address the problem of translation and interpretation across language barriers in national and international communications. It is an area where Information Technology can make a significant contribution, facilitating collaboration in Information Technology itself, and more generally. There is a need for research that addresses the need for communications, interpretation and translation in national and international contexts. There is a need to research the scope for Information Technology to provide an electronic environment in which, for example:

- Meetings could be held conveniently and effectively using appropriate telecommunication systems, with simultaneous interpretation by human or machine being provided by telecommunication from remote sources. This requires research on the human factors - especially the social psychology - of teleconferencing systems, building upon the work done in the 1970s and since. It also depends upon suitable developments in speech recognition systems, and further developments of automatic translation facilities.

- Voice Telephone conversations could be routed through simultaneous interpretation services provided by machines or humans to circumvent language problems during day-to-day voice communication.

- Electronic mail could be routed through machine translation or human translation services, to facilitate written communication across language barriers.

- Information accessed by telecommunication from remote databases could be routed through machine or human translation services in order that the user may receive the information in his or her preferred language.

Shared Human Factors facilities. As well as the language barriers which need to be overcome, there is a need to avoid unnecessary duplication of effort. A pooling of key resources could help to achieve this, and would also encourage synergy between the different elements that could be brought together from the different Member States. This would need to be done on a pre-competitive basis, and in that sense would be extending the spirit of ESPRIT and putting it, in regard to the facilities concerned, on a more permanent basis.

These facilities, in regard to Human Factors, could provide specialised equipment, techniques and expertise for Human Factors research and development activities. One might envisage, for example, a CAFE OF EVE (see the discussion of evaluation above) in each Member State that would provide a comprehensive, independent Human Factors Service to industry in that State. These facilities would communicate with one another, share information and developments, exchange personnel, and in other ways facilitate the development and harmonisation of Human Factors internationally throughout the European Community.

APPENDIX I:

CURRENT STATUS OF HUMAN FACTORS IN ESPRIT

INTRODUCTION

This appendix reflects the author's own understandings, opinions and interpretations. It draws on available documents issued by the Commission and on the author's direct involvement with ESPRIT, but the account is a personal one. It is intended to be accurate but the history and status of ESPRIT is complex and the account given may not agree in every respect with others, and should not be construed to be an official statement. The account provided here focusses on Human Factors. For recent brief accounts of the overall ESPRIT programme the reader is referred especially to Carpentier (1985) and Cadiou (1985).

Human Factors appears explicitly as part of the ESPRIT Subprogramme 4 on Office Systems. There are five subprogrammes in total within ESPRIT, as follows:

1. Advanced microelectronics
2. Software technology
3. Advanced information processing
4. Office systems
5. Computer integrated manufacturing.

Following the original Consultancy Studies which helped to provide an initial framework for the ESPRIT Programme, a small number of Preparatory Studies were funded in order to define and elaborate the key areas in more detail. Human Factors was identified as one of the key areas that needed to be addressed within the broad area of office systems, and the Human Factors Technology Centre in the U.K. jointly with Softlab in F.R. Germany conducted the Preparatory Study for that area. The study was designed to provide an overview of what the two partners from their industry perspective considered to be the state-of-the art in areas which they felt to be of particular importance in relation to the future development of electronic office systems, and to indicate what kind of research would be needed. Work on the Study effectively started in January of 1983 (following signature of contracts just before Christmas) and was effectively completed with delivery and presentation of the draft final report in April 1983. This book is based on that Preparatory Study.

Whilst the Preparatory Studies were being done, work in some areas of ESPRIT continued with the launching of a set of Pilot Studies which were to provide an initial model in some respects for the Main Programme to follow. It was felt possible to define these Pilot Studies in the areas concerned on the basis of existing knowledge prior to the relevant Preparatory Studies, the latter providing further definition and elaboration. In the case of Human Factors, however, it was felt that work should await completion of the Preparatory Study, and so Human Factors was not explicitly written into the Pilot Studies, although some projects necessarily had some aspects that could be considered to involve Human Factors to some extent.

Following completion of the Preparatory Study of Human Factors, and subsequent committee work, Human Factors was explicitly written into the Office Systems Subprogramme of the Main ESPRIT Programme which was launched in 1984.

Human Factors appears in the Office Systems Subprogramme in two ways. First, and most important, it appears explicitly as part of an area labelled "office systems science and human factors". Secondly, it forms an implicit aspect of the work done in some of the other areas. Five areas in total have been defined for the Office Systems Subprogramme, as follows:

1. Office systems science and human factors.

   The aim of the office systems science part of this is to analyse office activities in order to see how information technology could be applied. The area addresses professional and managerial work as well as clerical work, and is concerned particularly with the automation of functions, the application of knowledge-based methods, and support of judgemental tasks.

   The human factors part is concerned with improving understanding of the human aspects of office work in order to help ensure high performance, optimal working conditions, good organisation, and user acceptance.

2. Advanced workstations and human-machine interfaces

   This is concerned with establishing major new human-machine interface technologies, peripheral technologies and document representation technologies, as well as techniques for manipulating information in ways that are important for the development of advanced office workstations. The emphasis is very much on the "technical" aspects of this, but there is clearly a need to draw on relevant psychological human factors research done under ESPRIT or elsewhere.

3. Communication systems

This is concerned with developing the technical fundamentals in communication systems architecture, optical technologies, the management of resources connected by networks, and system aspects of value-added services.

4. Advanced multi-media storage and retrieval systems

The aim here is to acquire the system and applications expertise related to storage and retrieval of all forms of office information. The emphasis is again on the "technical" aspects but to achieve solutions that mesh in with the characteristics of the human operators of such systems success depends crucially upon adequate use of psychological human factors knowledge.

5. Integrated office information systems

This is concerned with checking the validity of the information concepts developed in the other parts of the Subprogramme, by establishing test beds, prototypes, and by other means. The CAFE OF EVE concept discussed in chapter 6 is clearly relevant here, as well as associated aspects of Human Factors evaluation.

Projects in each of these areas, as is the case for ESPRIT in general, fall into one or other of two somewhat ill-defined categories, labelled A and B. Type A projects are projects that are individually described in the ESPRIT Workplan. They have specified overall and intermediate objectives, and require constant perspectives. They usually require large resources, in both human and financial terms, and they usually require considerable infrastructure. Type B projects, on the other hand, are covered by "research themes" which are indicative but do not form an exhaustive listing. They usually require smaller resources, and there is somewhat less emphasis on systematic milestones and review cycles. Project proposals in either category can cover work for up to five years although initial contracts will normally be for shorter periods than this and a five-year project would normally require two or more sequential contracts. Funding is normally on a fifty-fifty basis, half of the funds coming from the Commission and half from the consortium doing the work.

OFFICE SYSTEMS SCIENCE AND HUMAN FACTORS

It is recognised that the understanding of office systems is patchy. There is no formal science of office automation. The main areas identified as needing research in this area of ESPRIT are: office systems analysis; office systems design; human factors; and the possible application of knowledge-based methods. The first three of these are separately defined within the "office systems science and human factors" area, but the work on application of knowledge-based methods is not treated separately. The research on the "analysis" aspects should be aimed at providing inputs to the more "design-oriented" aspects.

The inclusion of Human Factors into this part of the Subprogramme is seen to be essential for the effective use and broad acceptance of the envisaged systems and for their economic success. The Human Factors component of this part of the Subprogramme includes work on cognitive psychology as well as work structuring, qualification and training. Human Factors Laboratories are also seen to be important for providing centres of competence, acting in a catalytic manner to stimulate awareness and use of Human Factors, and offering possibilities for unbiased judgement about experimental systems and commercial products.

The key areas where Human Factors contributions are being made or would be important are as follows.

Human Factors

Human factors laboratories. An A-type project has been agreed in which several major industry partners are cooperating to establish a set of European Human Factors Laboratories where research can be conducted economically and fruitfully, where design guidelines can be developed, where human factors specialists can be trained, and where advice can be given to development laboratories.

The work currently defined includes investigation and development of a multimedia user-system interface that is optimal from a Human Factors point of view. The work will include an analysis of how people use information and for what purposes. User reactions to existing systems will be studied. How best to facilitate the learning of new systems will also be included in the research. The knowledge gained will be made available to European industry generally in two main ways. First, a software-based integrated decision-support system will be made available. Secondly, a broad programme of publications, seminars, workshops and consultancy activities will be organised.

Proposals were invited for the 1985 round that would contribute to the ongoing work.

Human-machine cognitive compatibility. A two-year, B-type project was started in 1984/5 to examine the feasibility of developing a software-based design aid to assist the designer in assessing the human cognitive compatibility of particular interface designs for comparative purposes. The deliverables will include the software package and user guide, design guidelines derived from validation trials, and a review of cognitive modelling.

No further proposals were invited on this topic in 1985.

Qualification and work. B-type proposals were invited for the 1985 round to study the impact of the introduction of office systems on the qualifications and skills of office workers. An important aim of this topic area would be to implement and evaluate methods for increasing user skill, especially in the sense of self-improvement by the user.

User aids and learning tools. B-type proposals were invited for the 1985 round to research methods for providing online learning and help functions, defined and tested from a Human Factors point of view. Special emphasis was put on the development of tools.

Human-machine interface specification language. B-type proposals were invited for the 1985 round to study the full range of cognitive and physical interfaces between humans and integrated office systems. The aim is to define a language for the specification of the human-machine interface that will increase the effectiveness and efficiency of the study and design of user interfaces.

Natural language interpretation and production. B-type proposals were invited for the 1985 round to study aspects of natural language usage in the office environment, in relation to office automation. This includes the parallel usage of a number of natural languages. The aim of this topic area is to develop guidelines for solving the problems identified. The work might include experiments or demonstrations of limited scope to illustrate particular solutions.

Office Systems Analysis

Operational and functional analysis of office requirements. Human Factors has a potentially important role to play by applying theory and methods from social and organisational psychology to the analysis of the office. However, proposals in this area will be checked against work that has already been done or agreed, and in particular a B-type project on the "Functional analysis of office requirements". This project is developing new methods to investigate and analyse office functions, and to assess key qualitative and quantitative benefits to be gained through the use of new office systems. It will provide guidelines for the evaluation of available office systems, and will support manufacturers' choice of facilities to be integrated into new systems.

Palm (1985) provides an account of the early stages of this work.

Benefits analysis. Both concrete and abstract benefits (e.g. cost as compared with job satisfaction) as well as financially non-quantifiable factors (e.g. speed as compared with flexibility) are the concern of this topic. The reference to job satisfaction illustrates one way in which Human Factors, especially occupational psychology in this case, could be expected to make a contribution to this area. B-type proposals were being invited for the 1985 round of proposals with the proviso that they would be checked against ongoing work.

Analysis of human tasks within the office. New B-type proposals were being invited for the 1985 round. The aim of such projects would be to produce a method for the analysis of human tasks within the office, in both qualitative and quantitative terms. The method would be used to examine a representative sample of office types and to predict the changes in task structure that could be expected to result from the introduction of integrated office systems.

Office Systems Design

Techniques for user interface design. This topic area is concerned with how to use techniques such as icons, windows, menu selection, voice command, and so forth, in the user interface. The topic area relates clearly to the concept of "species of interaction" discussed in Chapter 3, and is an area where cognitive psychologists and other human factors specialists could be expected to be able to make a significant contribution. B-type proposals were being invited for the 1985 round.

OTHER TOPIC AREAS WHERE HUMAN FACTORS IS RELEVANT

Advanced Workstations and Human-Machine Interfaces

The emphasis in this area is very much on the "technical" aspects. It is to be expected that the work will benefit from the Human Factors projects identified above, but in addition one might expect further, more specific Human Factors contributions to be made, especially in regard to the following topics:

- o Systems aspects of workstation design, which includes designing and implementing a prototype office workstation. Ergonomic and other Human Factors knowledge should be applied.

- o Advanced multi-media user interfaces. The work includes the design and development of an experimental input-output device as part of a multimedia integrated workstation. This includes providing a user-system dialogue to be used in simulations of office procedures, office routines, and advanced office tasks. The specification of such a dialogue would most appropriately be considered a Human Factors responsibility.

- Flat panel workstation design, including ergonomic aspects.

- Office interface languages. This involves the definition and implementation of languages for easy user-system interaction, aimed at the natural language environments in the European Community and other major linguistic regions. The work could benefit from linguistic, psycholinguistic, and other Human Factors contributions.

- Multi-media document manipulation. The Human Factors input here could be primarily in terms of a contribution towards the definition of high-level information manipulation functions, together with a contribution towards a language or procedure to enable the user to define the specific manipulations required.

- User to user multimedia communications. The aim here is to develop a prototype system and evaluate its effectiveness in various communications contexts. The prototype would be designed to improve the effectiveness of communication between persons in pairs and in groups, by facilitating appropriate use of voice, handwriting, dataprocessing, document display, and slow-scan video. The Human Factors contributions could usefully include specification of the user interface from the user's point of view, definition of the range of communications contexts, and design of the evaluation procedures.

An early account of some aspects of this work is provided by Naffah *et al*. (1985).

Advanced Multi-Media Storage and Retrieval Systems

As above, the emphasis in this area is also very much on the "technical" aspects. It is to be expected that the work will benefit from the Human Factors projects identified above, but in addition one might expect further, more specific Human Factors contributions to be made, especially in regard to the following topics:

- New information models. The work here includes research into new models of information that can deal adequately with all forms of office information. The models need to take account of the human aspects of information processing.

- Usage and needs. The work includes studies of the kinds of information handling that users will need to do in advanced electronic environments, and the research could include studies of the interactions between humans and prototype workstations in realistic user environments.

Early accounts of work related to this area are provided by Bansler *et al*. (1985), Fedeli *et al*. (1985), Flocon (1985), Horak, Tartonson and Coulouris (1985), and Nebbia and Sandri (1985).

Integrated Office Information Systems

The testing of prototypes against requirements that are representative of market conditions is perhaps the most important check on the relevance of the research done. Two broad areas have been defined under ESPRIT which relate to this, as follows.

The first area is concerned with designing, developing and evaluating advanced office system prototypes which are based on state-of-the-art components developed in Europe under ESPRIT or otherwise. The work should take adequate account of the results of the research in the "office systems science and human factors" area.

The second area is concerned with developing suitable environments or "test beds" for evaluating office system components and integrated office system prototypes. The evaluation environments should provide for both qualitative and quantitative evaluation in a variety of simulated offices and enterprises. This work should also draw on the work in the "office systems science and human factors" area.

Both A-type and B-type proposals were invited for the 1985 round.

FINAL COMMENTS

The topic areas indicated above are perhaps the most relevant to Human Factors that have been identified so far. However, Human Factors contributions to some other areas might also be valuable, and no doubt there are still other areas which have not been identified yet but which will become apparent as ESPRIT progresses.

Further, more detailed and more up to date information about the current status of ESPRIT can be obtained from the Commission of the European Communities Information Technologies and Telecommunications Task Force, provisional address: Rue de la Loi 200, B-1049 Brussels.

APPENDIX II:

KEY RESEARCH CENTRES

INTRODUCTION

This appendix provides the names and addresses of some key research centres. No attempt has been made to be comprehensive, but the list should prove a useful starting point for anyone new to the field who may wish to learn more about particular aspects of the field and perhaps build up their own network of contacts through a "snowballing" process that could begin with some of the institutions suggested here. There is no suggestion that if a particular institution does not happen to be listed here then it is not doing useful work.

The list is organised into a relatively small number of major topic areas corresponding to the organisation of the chapters in the body of the book. In some cases, an institution is listed only under one area when in fact it is doing work in other areas as well. The particular contact names suggested are often arbitrary. The purpose has been to provide a usable list that is not too long and not too complex. There is no suggestion that any institution or person included in the list accepts the framework used to organise the list.

The topic areas used are:

1 general

2 definition of the problem
- models of user-system interaction
- the psychophysiological context
- the organisational context
- functional analysis
- applications, e.g.:
  - database access
  - electronic mail and computer conferencing
  - word processing
- evaluation

3 species of interaction
- visual display ergonomics
- input-output techniques
- command languages
- menu techniques
- speech technology
- knowledge-based techniques
- dialogue design methodology

4 the user's model of the system
- design guidelines
- training and guidance
- adaptive interfaces

5 species of information
- graphics

1. GENERAL

AT&T Bell Laboratories
Holmdel
New Jersey 07733
U.S.A.

Dr Thomas M. Gruenenfelder

Bell-Northern Research
P.O. Box 3511, Station C
Ottowa
Canada K1Y 4H7

Dr Christopher Labrador

British Telecom Research Laboratories
Martlesham Heath
Ipswich
England

Dr Roy Gray

Fraunhofer Institut fur Arbeitswirtschaft und Organisation (IAO)
Stuttgart
F.R. Germany

Professor H-J. Bullinger

Gesellschaft fur Mathematik und Datenverarbeitung (GMD)
Bonn
D-5205 St Augustin
F.R. Germany

Dr Michael Paetau

General Electric Company (GEC)
Research Laboratories
East Lane
Wembley
Middlesex HA9 7PP
England

Mr Arthur Foster

IBM Thomas J. Watson Research Center
Yorktown Heights
New York 10598
U.S.A.

Dr John C. Thomas

Institut National de Recherche on Informatique et en Automatique (INRIA)
Domaine de Voluceau
Rocqueucourt
B.P. 105 78150 Le Chesnay
France

Dr D.L. Scapin

ITT Europe Human Factors Technology Centre
ITT Europe ESC-RC
Great Eastern House
Edinburgh Way
Harlow
Essex CM20 2BN
England

Dr Bruce Christie

Laboratoires de Marcoussis
Centres de Recherches de la Compagnie Generale d'Electricite
Route de Nozay
F-91460 Marcoussis
France

Dr B. Flocon

Loughborough University of Technology
Department of Human Sciences
Loughborough
Leicestershire
England

Professor Brian Shackel

Massachusetts Institute of Technology (MIT)
Architecture Machine Group
Cambridge
Massachusetts 02139
U.S.A.

Dr Richard Bolt

Siemens AG
User Acceptance Laboratory
Hofmannstrasse 51
D-8000 Munich 70
F.R. Germany

Dr Reinhard Helmreich

Softlab GmbH
Arabellastr. 13
D-8000 Muenchen 81
F.R. Germany

Mr. Klaus Schroeder

Tokyo Institute of Technology
Department of System Science
Yokohama
Japan

Dr S. Kohayashi

University College London
Ergonomics Unit
26 Bedford Way
London WC1
England

Dr John Long

University of Toronto
Department of Industrial Engineering
Ontario
Canada M5S 1A4

Professor Brian R. Gaines

Wang Laboratories
Lowell
Massachussetts
U.S.A.

Dr Jonathan Grudin

Xerox Palo Alto Research Center
3333 Coyote Hill Road
Palo Alto
California 94304
U.S.A.

Dr Stuart K. Card

Xerox Office Systems Division
3333 Coyote Hill Road
Palo Alto
California 94304
U.S.A.

Dr Jarrett K. Rosenberg

2. DEFINITION OF THE PROBLEM

2.1 Models of User-System Interaction

ITT Europe Human Factors Technology Centre
ITT Europe ESC-RC
Great Eastern House
Edinburgh Way, Harlow, Essex CM20 2BN
England

Dr Margaret M. Gardiner

Keith London Associates
Welwyn Garden City
Hertfordshire
England

Dr Marion Wells

Medical Research Council Applied Psychology Unit
15 Chaucer Road
Cambridge CB2 2EF
England

Dr Thomas R.G. Green

National Physical Laboratory
Teddington
Middlesex
England

Dr Dianne Murray

University of California
Institute for Cognitive Science
San Diego
La Jolla
California 92093
U.S.A.

Dr Mary Riley

University of Oulu
Institute of Data Processing Science
Linnanmaa
SF-90570 Oulu 57
Finland

Dr Juhani Iivari

University of Sheffield
MRC/ESRC Social and Applied Psychology Unit, Dept. of Psychology
Sheffield S10 2TN
England

Dr Stephen J. Payne

2.2 The Psychophysiological Context

Karolinska Institute
Stockholm
Sweden

Dr M. Frankenhauser

University of Illinois
Cognitive Psychophysiology Laboratory
Champagne
Illinois
U.S.A.

Professor E. Donchin

University of Southampton
Department of Psychology
Southampton SO9
England

Professor Anthony Gale

2.3 The Organisational Context

Chalmers University of Technology
HUMOR, Department of Information Processing
S-412 96 Goteberg
Sweden

Dr Clas-Olof Kall

Copenhagen School of Economics and Business Administration
Information Systems Research Group
10 Julius Thomsens Plads
DK-1925 Copenhagen V
Denmark

Dr Niels Bjorn-Andersen

London School of Economics
Houghton Street
London WC2A 2AE

Dr R.A. Hirschheim

Loughborough University of Technology
HUSAT Research Centre
'The Elms'
Elms Grove
Loughborough
Leicestershire LE11 1RG

Dr Ken D. Eason

Riso National Laboratory
Roskilde
Denmark DK 4000

Dr J. Rasmussen

University of Leuven
Faculty of Psychology and Educational Sciences
Leuven
Belgium

Professor G. de Cock

2.4 Functional Analysis

AT&T Bell Laboratories
Summit
New Jersey
U.S.A.

Dr Catherine R. Marshall

Dansk Datamatik Center
Lundtoftevej 1C
DK-2800 Lyngby
Denmark

Dr Steen U. Palm

Loughborough University of Technology
HUSAT Research Centre
'The Elms'
Elms Grove
Loughborough
Leicestershire LE11 1RG

Dr Ken Eason

State University of Geut
Laboratory of Applied Psychology
Pasteurlaan 2
B-9000. Geut
Belgium

Professor M. Buelens

The MITRE Corporation
Bedford
Massachussetts
U.S.A.

Dr Nancy C. Goodwin

University of California
Institute for Cognitive Science
San Diego
La Jolla
California 92093
U.S.A.

Dr Paul Smolensky

University of Southampton
Department of Psychology
Southampton SO9
England

Professor Anthony Gale

University of Tampere
P.O. Box 607
SF-33101 Tampere 10
Finland

Dr Hannu Kangassalo

Western Australian Institute of Technology
School of Computing and Quantitative Studies
Bentley
Western Australia 6102

Dr Bernard C. Glasson

2.5 Applications

Database Access:

Bell Communications Research Incorporated
Juniper Plaza
Route 9
Freehold
New Jersey 07728
U.S.A.

Dr Carla J. Springer

IBM Entry Systems Division
P.O. Box 1328
Boca Raton
Florida 33432

Dr Ila J. Elson

Electronic Mail and Computer Conferencing:

Gesellschaft fur Mathematik und Datenverarbeitung (GMD)
P.O. Box 1240
D-5205 St Augustin
F.R. Germany

Mrs Uta Pankoke-Babatz

Loughborough University of Technology
Department of Human Sciences
Loughborough
Leicestershire
England

Dr D.J. Pullinger

National Computing Centre
Office Systems Division
Oxford Road
Manchester M1 7ED
England

Dr Paul Wilson

QZ Computer Center
Box 27322
S-102 54 Stockholm
Sweden

Dr Jacob Palme

University of Birmingham
Centre for Computing and Computer Science
Birmingham
England

Dr W.P. Dodd

Word Processing:

IBM Thomas J. Watson Research Center
Computer Science Department
Yorktown Heights
New York 10598
U.S.A.

Dr John M. Carroll

Xerox Palo ALto Research Center
Palo Alto
California
U.S.A.

Dr Stuart K. Card

2.6 Evaluation

Burroughs Corporation
Mission Viejo
California
U.S.A.

Dr Thomas S. Tullis

CCETT
Research Department ESA
BP.59 35510 Cesson-Sevigne
France

Dr Francis Kretz

ELLEMTEL
Utvecklings Aktiebolag
ALvsjo
Sweden

Dr Oleg de Bachtin

Free University of Berlin
Department of Psychology
Berlin
F.R. Germany

Professor W. Schonpflug

IBM General Products Division
Human Factors Department
76V/312 Tucson
Arizona 85744
U.S.A.

Dr Paul D. Tynan

New York University
Alternate Media Center
725 Broadway
New York
New York 10003
U.S.A.

Professor Martin C.J. Elton

The John Hopkins University
Communications Research Laboratory
Suites 302 and 303
7402 York Road
Baltimore
Maryland 21204
U.S.A.

Professor Alphonse Chapanis

University of California
Institute for Cognitive Science
San Diego
La Jolla
California 92093
U.S.A.

Dr Liam Bannon

University of York
Department of Psychology
York
England

Dr Nick Hammond

3 SPECIES OF INTERACTION

3.1 Visual Display Ergonomics

Human Factors Engineering
University OEH School of Medicine
PO ORIO
Yahata Nishi Ku Kitakyushu
807 Japan

Professor Kageyu Noro

Osaka University
Faculty of Engineering Sciences
Toyonaka
Osaka
Japan 560

Dr Hiroshi Tamura

Medical Research Council Applied Psychology Unit
15 Chaucer Road
Cambridge CB2 2EF
England

Dr Arnold Wilkins

The Pennsylvania State University
Department of Industrial and Management Systems Engineering
University Park
PA
U.S.A.

Dr Jeffrey L. Harpster

University of California
Section on Medical Information Science
San Francisco
California 94143
U.S.A.

Dr Dennis J. Streveler

3.2 Input-Output Techniques

Brighton Polytechnic
Department of Computing and Cybernetics
Brighton
England

Dr C.A. Higgins

IBM
Austin
Texas 78758
U.S.A.

Dr John Karat

Microtel Pacific Research, Ltd.
Burnaby
British Columbia
Canada

Dr M. Francas

University of Dundee
Dundee
Scotland

Dr R. Dye

University of Southampton
Department of Electronics
Southampton SO9
England

Dr A.C. Downton

University of Tokyo
Department of Information Science
Tokyo
Japan

Dr Takeshi Okadome

University of Toronto
Computer Systems Research Group
Toronto
Ontario M5S 1A4
Canada

Dr Martin Lamb

3.3 Command Languages

Bell Communications Research
Murray Hill
New Jersey
U.S.A.

Dr Louis M. Gomez

City of London Polytechnic
Department of Information Technology
Old Castle Street
London E1 7NT
England

Dr Julian Newman

Medical Research Council Applied Psychology Unit
15 Chaucer Road
Cambridge CB2 2EF
England

Dr Phil Barnard

3.4 Menu Techniques

AT&T Bell Laboratories
Murray Hill
New Jersey 07974
U.S.A.

Dr Gary Perlman

Forschungsinstitut fur Anthropotechnik
Wachtberg-Werthhoven
F.R. Germany

Dr J. Kaster

University of Waikato
Hamilton
New Zealand

Dr M.D. Apperley

3.5 Speech Technology

City University of New York
Psychology Department, Hunter College
New York, N.Y.
U.S.A.

Dr Martin Chodorow

CSELT
Via G. Reiss Romoli, 274
10148 Torino
Italy

Dr Luciano Nebbia

University of Southampton
Department of Electronics and Information Engineering
Southampton SO9 5NH
England

Dr R.I. Damper

3.6 Knowledge-Based Techniques

Battelle-Institut
Am Romerhof 35, Postfach 90 01 60
D-6000 Frankfurt/Main
F.R. Germany

Dr M.S. Gwiebner

Institut fur Informatik
University of Stuttgart
Herdweg 51
D-7000 Stuttgart

Dr Joachim Laubsch

Institute of Interdisciplinary Research
Faculty of Engineering
University of Tokyo
Tokyo

Dr S. Ohsuga

Institute di Matematica, Informatic e Sistomatica
University of Udine
Udine

Professor G. Guida

University of Edinburgh
Department of Machine Intelligence
Edinburgh

Professor D. Michie

York University
Department of Computer Science
4700 Keele Street
Downsview
Ontario M3J 1P3
Canada

Dr Mildred L.G. Shaw

3.7 Dialogue Design Methodology

Leicester Polytechnic
Human-Computer Interface Research Unit
P.O. Box 143
Leicester
England

Dr Ernest Edmonds

PA Management Consultants
Cambridge Laboratory
Melbourn
Royston
Hertfordshire SG8 6DP
England

Dr Norman Schofield

Virginia Polytechnic and State University
Department of Computer Science
Blacksburg
Virginia 24061
U.S.A.

Dr H. Rex Hartson

4 THE USER'S MODEL OF THE SYSTEM

4.1 Design Guidelines

Loughborough University of Technology
HUSAT Research Centre
'The Elms'
Elms Grove
Loughborough
Leicestershire LE11 1RG

Dr Arthur Gardner

The MITRE Corporation
Bedford
Massachussetts 01730
U.S.A.

Dr Sidney L. Smith

University of California
Institute of Human Learning
Berkeley
California 94720

Dr Darlene Clement

University of York
Department of Computer Science
York YO1 5DD
England

Dr Harold Thimbleby

4.2 Training and Guidance

Brunal University
Centre for the Study of Human Learning
Brunel
Uxbridge
England

Dr Sheila Harri-Augstein

Open University
Institute of Educational Technology
Milton Keynes
England

Dr Ann Jones

Philips Research Laboratories
Redhill
Surrey
England

Dr D.E. Penna

Virginia Polytechnic Institute and State University
Blacksburg
Virginia
U.S.A.

Dr Robert C. Williges

4.3 Adaptive Interfaces

Leicester Polytechnic
Leicester
England

Dr David Benyon

Loughborough University of Technology
HUSAT Research Centre
'The Elms'
Elms Grove
Loughborough
Leicestershire LE11 1RG

Dr H.S. Maskery

University of Strathclyde
Department of Computer Science
Glasgow G1 1XH
Scotland

Dr J.L. Alty

5 SPECIES OF INFORMATION

5.1 Graphics

University of Edinburgh
EdCAAD, Department of Architecture
Edinburgh
Scotland

Dr Aart Bijl

University of Hull
Department of Geography
Hull HU6 7RX
England

Dr M. Visvalingam

University of Warwick
Department of Engineering
Coventry CV4 7AL
England

Dr Neil Storey

REFERENCES

Anderson, J.R. (1972)
FRAN: A simulation model of free recall. In G.H. Bower (Ed.) The psychology of learning and motivation: advances in research and theory, Vol. 5. New York: Academic Press, 1972.

Argyle, M., Furnham, A., & Graham, J.A. (1981)
Social situations. Cambridge: Cambridge University Press.

Arnheim, R. (1969)
Visual thinking. Berkley: University of California Press.

Atwood, M.E.I. & Ramsey, H.R. (1979)
Human factors in computer systems: a review of the literature. Englewood, Colorado: Science Applications Inc.

Bansler, J., Bogh, T., Bruce, D., Hansen, H., Harper, D., McAlpine, G., Morrissey, J., Restorick, F.M., Rivkin, L.S., Sherwood-Smith, M., Smeaton, A.F., & Van Rijsbergen, C.J. (1985)
Filing and retrieval of unstructured information: some system considerations. In: J. Roukens & J.F. Renuart (eds.) (1985) ESPRIT '84: status report of ongoing work. Amsterdam: North-Holland Publishing Company for the Commission of the European Communities.

Barber, G. R. (1980)
Reasoning about change in knowledgeable office systems. Proceedings of the 1st Annual National Conference on Artificial Intelligence, Stanford.

Bartlett, F.C. (1932)
Remembering. Cambridge: Cambridge University Press.

Birchall, D.W. and Hammond, V.J. (1981)
Tommorrow's office today: managing technological change. London: Business Books, Hutchinson Publishing Group.

Bolt, R. A. (1981)
Speech at the interface. Proceedings of the Conference of the Canadian Man-Computer Communications Society, Waterloo, Ontario, 10 - 12 June 1981.

Bolt, R.A. (1982)
Eyes at the interface. Proceedings of a Conference on Human Factors in Computer Systems, Gathersbury, USA, 1982, pp. 360-362.

Bower, G.H., & Winzenz, D. (1970)
Comparison of associative learning strategies. Psychonomic Science, 20, 119-120.

Bradord, W. (1982)
Comparing professional work stations - hot prospect. Computer World, 16(36A), September, pp. 67 -70.

Cadiou, J.M. (1985)
An introduction to the ESPRIT programme. In: J. Roukens & J.F. Renuart (eds.) (1985) ESPRIT '84: status report of ongoing work. Amsterdam: North-Holland Publishing Company for the Commission of the European Communities.

Cakir, A., Hart, D.J., & Stewart, T.M.F. (1980)
Visual display terminals: a manual covering ergonomics, workplace design, health and safety and task organisation. Chichester: John Wiley & Sons.

Card, S.K., English, W.K., & Burr, B.J. (1978)
Evaluation of mouse, rate-controlled isometric joystick, step keys, and text keys for text selection on a CRT. Ergonomics, 21, 601-613.

Card, S.K., Moran, T.P., & Newell, A. (1983)
The psychology of human-computer interaction. London/New Jersey: Lawrence Erlbaum Associates.

Carpentier, M. (1985)
Opening address to the ESPRIT technical week. In: J. Roukens & J.F. Renuart (eds.) (1985) ESPRIT '84: status report of ongoing work. Amsterdam: North-Holland Publishing Company for the Commission of the European Communities.

Champness, B.G., & De Alberdi, M. (1981)
Measuring subjective reactions to teletext page design. Technical Report, Alternate Media Center, New York University.

Champness, B.G., & Ikhlef, A. (1982)
Subjective reactions and performance of teletext viewers in response to graphics, colored text. Technical report, Alternate Media center, New York University.

Christie, B. (1985) (ed.)
Human factors of information technology in the office. Chichester: John Wiley and Sons.

Cohen, B.G.F. (1984) (ed.)
Human aspects in office automation. Amsterdam: Elsevier Science Publishers.

Cranach, M. von, Kalbermatten, U., Indermuhle, K., and Gugler, B. (1982)
Goal-directed action. London: Academic Press.

Christie, B. (1981)
Face to file communication. Chichester/New York: John Wiley and Sons.

Collins, A.M., & Quillian, M.R. (1972)
How to make a language user. In E. Tulving and W. Donaldson (Eds.) Organization of memory. New York: Academic Press, 1972.

Damper, R.I., Lambourne, A.D., & Guy, D.P. (1984)
Speech input as an adjunct to keyboard entry in television subtitling. INTERACT '84: first IFIP conference on 'human-computer interaction', Volume 1. Amsterdam: Elsevier Science Publishers, pp. 43-48.

Dixon, M. (1981)
Algorithms and selective attention. Memory and Cognition, 9(2), 177-184.

Doswell, A. (1983)
Office automation. Chichester: John Wiley & Sons.

Downton, A.C., & Brooks, C.P. (1984)
Automated machine shorthand transcription in commercial applications. INTERACT '84: first IFIP conference on 'human-computer interaction', Volume 2. Amsterdam: Elsevier Science Publishers, pp. 80-85.

Durding, B.M., Becker, C.A., & Gould, J.D. (1977)
Data organization. Human Factors, 19(1), 1-14.

Durrett, J., & Trezona, J. (1982)
How to use colour graphics effectively. BYTE, 7(4), April.

Dye, R., Newell, A.F., & Arnott, J.L. (1984)
An adaptive editor for shorthand transcription systems. INTERACT '84: first IFIP conference on 'human-computer interaction', Volume 2. Amsterdam: Elsevier Science Publishers, pp. 92-96.

Dzida, W., Herda, S., & Itzfeld, W.D. (1978)
User-perceived quality of interactive systems. IEEE Transactions on SW-Engineering, SE-4(4), July.

Easterby, R. & Zwaga, H. (1984)
Information design: the design and evaluation of signs and printed material. Chichester: John Wiley & Sons.

Edmonds, E.A., & Guest, S.P. (1984)
The SYNICS2 user interface manager. INTERACT '84: first IFIP conference on 'human-computer interaction', Volume 1. Amsterdam: Elsevier Science Publishers, pp. 53-56.

Ellis, C.A. (1979)
Information control nets: a mathematical model of office information flow. Proceedings of a Conference on Simulation, Measurement and Modeling of Computer Systems, Boulder Colorado, Association for Computing Machinery, 225-239.

Ellis, W., & Miller, D. (1981)
Left and wrong in adverts: neuropsychological correlates of aesthetic preference. British Journal of Psychology, 72, 225-229.

Emblkey, D.W., & Nagy, G. (1981)
Behavioural aspects of text editors. ACM Computing Surveys, 13(1), March.

Engel, G.H., Groppuso, J., Lowenstein, R.A., & Traub, W.G. (1979)
An office communication system. IBM System Journal, 18(3), 402-431.

Erickson, M.H., & Rossi, E.L. (1979)
Hypnotherapy: an exploratory casebook. New York: Irvington Publishers, Inc. (Halsted Press Division of John Wiley & Sons).

Feigenbaum, E.A. & McCorduck, P. (1983)
The fifth generation: artificial intelligence and Japan's computer challenge to the world. London/California: Addison-Welsely.

Fikes, R.E., & Henderson, A.D. (1980)
On supporting the use of procedures in office work. Proceedings of the 1st Annual National Conference on Artificial Intelligence, Stanford.

Finseth, C.A. (1982)
Managing Words. BYTE, 7(4), April.

Flocon, B. (1985)
Multimedia user interface at office workstation: speech recognition. In J. Roukens and J.F. Renuart (eds.) ESPRIT '84: status report on ongoing work. Amsterdam: North-Holland for the Commission of the European Communities, pp. 315-325.

Flowers, J.H., Polansky, M.L.M., & Kerl, S. (1981)
Familiarity, redundancy and the spatial control of visual attention. Journal of Experimental Psychology: Human Perception and Performance, 7(1), 157-166.

Foster, J.J., & Bruce, M. (1982)
Looking for entries in videotex tables: a comparison of four color formats. Journal of Applied Psychology, 57(5), 611-615.

Francas, M., Goodman, D., & Dickinson, J. (1984)
Input devices for public videotex services. INTERACT '84: first IFIP conference on 'human-computer interaction', Volume 2. Amsterdam: Elsevier Science Publishers, pp. 213-217.

Friend, D. (1983)
Graphics for managers: the distributed approach. Datamation, 29(1), 76-96.

Firita, R., Scofield J., & Shaw, A. (1982)
Document formatting systems: surveys concepts and issues. ACM Computing Surveys, 14(3), September.

Gale, A. (1973)
The psychophysiology of individual differences: studies of extraversion and the EEG. In P. Kline (ed.) New approaches in psychological measurement. Chichester: John Wiley & Sons.

Gale, A., & Edwards, J.A. (1985)
Individual differences. In M.G.H. Coles, E. Donchin, & S.W. Porges (eds.) Psychophysiology: systems, processes, and applications. New York: Guilford.

Garnham, H.J.A. (1981)
An investigation of the nature of abstract concepts. Memory and Cognition, 9(2).

Geiselman, R.E. & Samet, M.G. (1980)
Summarizing military information: an application of schema theory. Human Factors, 22(6), 693-705.

Gentner, D. & Stevens, A.L. (1983)
Mental models. Hillsdale, New Jersey: Lawrence Erlbaum Associates.

Giuliano, V.E. (1982)
The mechanization of office work. Scientific American, February.

Goldberg, A. (1981)
Introducing the Smalltalk-80 system. BYTE, 6(8), August.

Goldstein, I.P., & Bobrow, D.G. (1980)
Descriptions for a programming environment. Proceedings of the 1st Annual National Conference on Artificial Intelligence, Stanford.

Grandjean, E., Nishiyama, K., Hunting, W., & Piderman, M. A. (1982)
Laboratory study on preferred and imposed setting of a VDT workstation. Behaviour and Information Technology, 1(3), 289-302.

Grandjean, E. & Vigliani, E. (1982) (eds.)
Ergonomic aspects of visual display terminals. London: Taylor and Francis.

Hacker, W. (1978)
Allgemeine arbeits- und ingenieurpsychologie. Bern: Huber Verlag.

Haller, R., Mutschler, H., & Voss, M. (1984)
Comparison of input devices for correction of typing errors in office systems. INTERACT '84: first IFIP conference on 'human-computer interaction', Volume 2. Amsterdam: Elsevier Science Publishers, pp. 218-223.

Hammer, M., & Kunin, J.S. (1980)
Design principles of an office specification language. Proceedings of the National Computer Conference, 49, 541-548.

Harris, L. (1982)
The four obstacles to end user access. Proceedings of the Fifth Generation Conference, London, July.

Hartson, H.R., Johnson, D.H., & Ehrich, R.W. (1984)
A human-computer dialogue management system. INTERACT '84: first IFIP conference on 'human-computer interaction', Volume 1. Amsterdam: Elsevier Science Publishers, pp. 57-61.

Hattke, W., Staehle, W.H., & Sydow, J. (1981)
Situative Analyse der Bildschirmarbeit. Zeitschrift fur Organisation, 50(4), 215-223.

Hattke, W., Staehle, W.H., & Sydow, J. (1981)
Entwicklungsstufen der Buroautomation Institut Fur Unternehmensfuhrung, Fachbereich Wirtschaftswissenschaft, Freie Universitat Berlin, Arbeitspapier Nr. 19/81 ISBN 3 88298 039 0 Berlin, November.

Henkel, T. (1981)
Talking computers still science fiction. Computerworld, 17, January.

Hewitt, C., Attardi, G., & Simi, M. (1980)
Knowledge embedding in the description system Omega. Proceedings of the 1st Annual National Conference on Artificial Intelligence, Stanford.

Higgins, C.A., & Whitrow, R.J. (1984)
On-line cursive script recognition. INTERACT '84: first IFIP conference on 'human-computer interaction', Volume 2. Amsterdam: Elsevier Science Publishers, pp. 140-144.

Hochberg, J. (1970)
Components of literacy: speculations and exploratory research. In H. Leven and J.P. Williams (Eds.) Basic studies in reading. New York: Basic Books.

Hochberg, J. (1972)
The representation of things and people. In E.H. Gombrich, J. Hochberg & M. Black (eds.) Art, perception and reality. Baltimore: Johns Hopkins University Press.

Horak, W., Tartonson, F., & Coulouris, G. (1985)
Handling of mixed text/image/voice documents based on a standardized office document architecture. In: J. Roukens & J.F. Renuart (eds.) (1985) ESPRIT '84: status report of ongoing work. Amsterdam: North-Holland Publishing Company for the Commission of the European Communities.

Iivari, J., & Koskela, E. (1984)
On the modelling of human-computer interaction as the interface between the user's work activity and the information system. INTERACT '84: first IFIP conference on 'human-computer interaction', Volume 1. Amsterdam: Elsevier Science Publishers, pp. 150-157.

Ingalls, D.H.H. (1981)
Design principles behind Smalltalk. BYTE,6(8), August.

Irby, C., Bergsteinsson, L., Moran, T., Newman, W., & Tesler, L. (1977)
A methodology for user interface design. Systems Development Division, Xerox Corporation, January 1977.

Jarrett, D. (1982)
The electronic office: a management guide to the office of the future. Aldershot: Gower Publishing Company Ltd.

Johnson-Laird, P.N. (1983)
Mental models. Cambridge: Cambridge University Press.

Jong, S. (1982)
Designing a text editor? The user comes first. BYTE,7(4), April.

Karat, J., McDonald, J.E., & Anderson, M. (1984)
A comparison of selection techniques: touch panel, mouse and keyboard. INTERACT '84: first IFIP conference on 'human-computer interaction', Volume 2. Amsterdam: Elsevier Science Publishers, pp. 149-153.

Kennedy, T.C.S. (1975)
Some behavioural factors affecting the training of naive users of an interactive computer system. International Journal of Man-Machine Studies, 7, 817-834.

La Berge, D. and Samuels, S.J. (1974)
Towards a theory of automatic information processing in reading. Cognitive Psychology, 6, 293-323.

Labrador, C., & Pai, D. (1984)
Experiments in speech interaction with conventional data services. INTERACT '84: first IFIP conference on 'human-computer interaction', Volume 1. Amsterdam: Elsevier Science Publishers, pp. 104-108.

Lamb, M.R., & Buckley, V. (1984)
New techniques for gesture-based dialogue. INTERACT '84: first IFIP conference on 'human-computer interaction', Volume 2. Amsterdam: Elsevier Science Publishers, pp. 145-148.

Lea, W.A. (Ed.) (1980)
Trends in speech recognition. London: Prentice Hall

Lea, W.A. (1983)
Computer recognition of speech. Santa Barbara: Speech Science Publications.

Lea, W.A. (1983)
Selection, designing and using speech recognition systems. Santa Barbara: Speech Science Publications.

Lebensold, J., Radhakrishnan, T., & Jaworski, W.M. (1982)
A modelling tool for office information systems. In J.O. Limb (eds.) *SIGOA Conference on Office Information Systems*, Association for Computing Machinery, Reference No. 0-89791-075-3/82/006/0141, Order No. 611820, 141-152.

Leedham, C.G., Downton, A.C., & Brooks, C.P. (1984)
On-line acquisition of Pitman's handwritten shorthand as a means of rapid data entry. *INTERACT '84: first IFIP conference on 'human-computer interaction'*, Volume 2. Amsterdam: Elsevier Science Publishers, pp. 86-91.

Mantei, M.M. (1982)
Disorientation behaviour in person-computer interaction. PH.D Thesis. University of Southern California.

Marcus, A. (1983)
InterGraphics '83: tutorial sessions A4. World Computer Graphics Association, Inc., 2033 M Street N.W. Suite 399, Washington, D.C. 20036, U.S.A.

Mayer, R.E. (1979)
Denken and problemlosen. Berlin: Springer Verlag.

Meyrowitz, N., & Van Dam, A. (1982)
Interactive editing systems. *ACM computing surveys*, *14*(3), September.

Miller, I.S.T. (1981)
Preferred height and angle settings of CRT and keyboard for a display station input task. *Proceedings of the 25th Human Factors Society Meeting*, Rochester, USA., pp. 492-496.

Miller, J. (1981)
Global precedence in attention and decision. *Journal of Experimental Psychology: Human Perception and Performance*, *7*(6), 1161-1174.

Miller, L.A. (1980)
Project EPISTLE: a system for the automatic analysis of business correspondence. Proceedings of the 1st Annual National Conference on Artificial Intelligence, Stanford.

Miller, R.B. (1968)
Response time in man-computer transactions. AFIPS Proceedings of the Spring Joint Computer Conference, 33(1), pp 267-277.

Miller, G.A., Galanter, E., & Pribram, K.H. (1960)
Plans and the structure of behavior. New York: Holt.

Mills, M.I. (1982)
A study of the human response to pictorial representations on Telidon. Technical Report from the Department of Communications, Ottawa.

Mohl, R. (1980)
The interactive movie map applications of interactive television and the video disc. 1980 Midcon Professional Program.

Monk, A. (1984)
Fundamentals of human-computer interaction. London: Academic Press.

Murray, D., & Bevan, N. (1984)
The social psychology of computer conversations. INTERACT '84: first IFIP conference on 'human-computer interaction'. Amsterdam: Elsevier Science Publishers, pp. 268-273.

Muter, P., Latremoville, S.A., Treurniet, W.C., & Beam, P. (1982)
Extended reading of continuous text on television screens. Human Factors, 24(5), 501-508.

Naffah, N. (ed.) (1982)
Office information systems. Amsterdam: North Holland Publishing Company.

Naffah, N., Kempen, G., Rohmer, J., Steels, L., & Tsichritzis, D. (1985)
Intelligent workstation in the office: state of the art and future perspectives. In J. Roukens and J.F. Renuart (eds.) ESPRIT '84: status report on ongoing work. Amsterdam: North-Holland for the Commission of the European Communities, pp. 365-378.

Nebbia, L. & Sandri, S. (1985)
Multimedia user interface at the office workstation speech interface - speech synthesis. In J. Roukens and J.F. Renuart (eds.) ESPRIT '84: status report on ongoing work. Amsterdam: North-Holland for the Commission of the European Communities, pp. 327-335.

Negroponte, N. (unpublished)
The impact of optical videodiscs on film making. Unpublished paper.

Norman, D.A. (1984)
Four stages of user activities. INTERACT '84: first IFIP conference on 'human-computer interaction'. Amsterdam: Elsevier Science Publishers, pp. 81-85.

Nutt, G.J., & Ricci, P.A. (1981)
Quinault: an office modeling system. IEEE Computer Magazine, 14(5), 41-57.

Olson, M.H., Lucas, H.C. (1982)
The impact of office automation on the organization: some implications for research and practice. ACM Communications, 25(11), November.

Otway, H.J. & Peltu, M. (1983) (eds.)
New office technology: human and organizational aspects, A publication from the INSIS (Inter-institutional Integrated Services Information System) Programme of the Commission of the European Communities. London: Frances Pinter for the Commission of the European Communities.

Palm, S.U. (1985)
An office investigation and analysis method. In: J. Roukens & J.F. Renuart (eds.) (1985) ESPRIT '84: status report of ongoing work. Amsterdam: North-Holland Publishing Company for the Commission of the European Communities.

Pava, C. (1983)
Managing new office technology: an organizational strategy. London: Collier Macmillan.

Payne, S.J. (1984)
Task-action grammars. In: INTERACT '84: first IFIP conference on 'human-computer interaction'. Amsterdam: Elsevier Science Publishers.

Porter, L.W. & Roberts, K.H. (1976)
Communication in organizations, In: M.D. Dunnette (Ed.) Handook of industrial and organizational psychology. Chicago: Rand McNally College Publishing Company, 1976, pp. 1553-1590.

Prien, E.P. & Ronan, W.W. (1971)
Job analysis: a review of research findings. Personnel Psychology, 24, 371-396.

Reenskaug, T.M.H. (1981)
User-oriented descriptions of Smalltalk systems. BYTE, August.

Reisner, P. (1981)
Human factor studies of database query languages: a survey and assessment. ACM Computing Surveys, 13(1), March.

Richards, M.A., & Underwood, K.M. (1984)
How should people and computers speak to each other? INTERACT '84: first IFIP conference on 'human-computer interaction', Volume 1. Amsterdam: Elsevier Science Publishers, pp. 33-36.

Riley, M., & O'Malley, C. (1984)
Planning nets: a framework for analyzing user-computer interactions. INTERACT '84: first IFIP conference on 'human-computer interaction'. Amsterdam: Elsevier Science Publishers, pp. 86-91.

Robertson, G. McCracken, D. & Newell, A. (1981)
The ZOG approach to man-machine communication. International Journal of Man-Machines Studies, 14, 461-488.

Robson, D. (1981)
Object-oriented software systems. BYTE, 6(8), August.

Rochester, N., Bequaert, F.C., & Sharp, E. (1978)
The chord keyboard. IEEE Computer, December.

Rosch, E. Mervis, C.B., Gray, W.D., Johnson, D.M., & Boyes-Braem, P. (1976)
Basic objects in natural categories. Cognitive Psychology, 382-439.

Roukens, J. & Renuart, J.F. (1985)
ESPRIT '84: status report of ongoing work. Amsterdam: North-Holland for the Commission of the European Communities.

Samet, M.G. & Geiselman, R.E. (1981)
Developing guidelines for summarizing information. Human Factors, 23(6), 727-736.

Scannel, T.J. (1982)
Video disks - the race is on! Computer World, 16(36A), September, 75 - 78.

Scarrott, G.G. (1979)
From computing slave to knowledgeable servant: the evolution of computers. Proceedings of the Royal Society, London, 369A, 1-30.

Schnupp, P., & Floyd, C. (1976)
Software. Berlin: Walter de Gruyter.

Schunemann, T.M., & Ullmer, W. (1982)
A framework for the realization of uniform user interfaces. Angewandte Informatik, November.

Shirai, Y. (1982)
Image processing for data capture. IEEE Computer, 15(11), November.

Short, J., Williams, E. & Christie, B. (1976)
The social psychology of telecommunications. Chichago/New York: John Wiley and Sons.

Sime, M.E. & Coombs, M.J. (1983)
Designing for human-computer communication. London/New York: Academic Press.

Simpson, H. (1982)
A human factors style guide for program design. BYTE, 7(4), April.

Smith, D.C., Irby, C., Kimball, R., & Verplank, B. (1982)
Designing the Star user interface. BYTE, 7(4), April.

Smith, E.E., Shoben, E.J., & Rips, L.J. (1974)
Structures and process in semantic memory: a featural model for semantic decisions. Psychological Review, 81, 214-241.

Spence, R., & Apperley, M. (1982)
Data base navigation: an office environment for the professional. Behaviour and Information Technology, 1(1).

Storey, N., & Craine, J.F. (1984)
Interactive stereoscopic computer graphic display systems. INTERACT '84: first IFIP conference on 'human-computer interaction', Volume 1. Amsterdam: Elsevier Science Publishers, pp. 382-387.

Sutherland, S. (1980)
Prestel and the user. London: Central Office of Information.

Thomas, J.C., Rosson, M.B., & Chodorow, M. (1984)
Human factors and synthetic speech. INTERACT '84: first IFIP conference on 'human-computer interaction', Volume 1. Amsterdam: Elsevier Science Publishers, pp. 37-42.

Thorndyke, P.W. (1977)
Cognitive structures in comprehension and memory of narrative discourse. Cognitive Psychology, 9, 77-110.

Tsichritzis, D., Thanos, C., Rabitti, F., Christidoulakis, S., Gibbs, S., Bertino, E., Fedeli, A., Faloutsos, C., & Economopoulos, P. (1985)
Design issues of a file server for multimedia documents. In: J. Roukens & J.F. Renuart (eds.) (1985) ESPRIT '84: status report of ongoing work. Amsterdam: North-Holland Publishing Company for the Commission of the European Communities.

Van de Ven, A.H., & Ferry, D.L. (1980)
Measuring and assessing organizations. New York: John Wiley & Sons.

Visick, D.S., Johnson, P., & Long, J.B. (1984)
The use of simple speech recognisers in industrial applications. INTERACT '84: first IFIP conference on 'human-computer interaction', Volume 1. Amsterdam: Elsevier Science Publishers, pp. 99-103.

Wason, P.C. & Evans, J. St. B.T. (1975)
Dual processes in reasoning? Cognition, 3, 141-154.

Wells, M. (1984)
Representing the user's model of an interactive system. INTERACT '84: first IFIP conference on 'human-computer interaction', Volume 1. Amsterdam: Elsevier Science Publishers, pp. 145-149.

Weizenbaum, J. (1966)
Eliza - a computer program for the study of natural language communication between man and machine. ACM Communications, 9(1), January.

Wilkins, A. (1984)
Visual discomfort and cathode ray tube displays. INTERACT '84: first IFIP conference on human-computer interaction. Amsterdam: Elsevier Science Publishers, 76-80.

Williams, G. (1983)
The Lisa computer system. BYTE, February.

Wright, P. (1977)
Presenting technical information: a survey of research findings. International Science, 6, 93-134.

Xerox Learning Research Group (1981)
The Smalltalk-80 System. BYTE, 6(8), August.

Zisman, M.D. (1982)
Ease of use - What does it mean? Computer World, 16(36A), September.

SUBJECT INDEX

The index is provided in two forms:

- Context-provided (p. 261). In this index, entries are listed according to the sections of the chapters in which they appear. This has the advantage that the meaning of the entry can usually be inferred from its context, but it requires visual scanning of the index to find entries of interest.

- Alphabetical (p. 267). This more conventional form of the index lists the entries in alphabetical order. This makes it easy to see if a particular word or phrase is listed, but means that alternative wordings are difficult to find.

The two forms of the index are related by the entry (E) numbers, so that cross-referencing from the alphabetical to the context-provided index is possible, which may help to disambiguate some entries.

Context-Provided

page

Alphabetical